# A DOOR IN THE HIVE
# EVENING TRAIN

# A DOOR IN
# THE HIVE

## Denise
## Levertov

# EVENING
# TRAIN

BLOODAXE BOOKS

This edition first published 1993 by
Bloodaxe Books Ltd,
P.O. Box 1SN,
Newcastle upon Tyne NE99 1SN.

ISBN: 1 85224 159 4

*A Door in the Hive* first published 1989
and *Evening Train* first published 1992
by New Directions Publishing Corporation, New York.
Copyright © Denise Levertov
1984, 1987, 1988, 1989, 1990, 1991, 1992, 1993.

Bloodaxe Books Ltd acknowledges
the financial assistance of Northern Arts.

Author photograph by David Geier.

Cover printing by J. Thomson Colour Printers Ltd, Glasgow.

Printed in Great Britain by
the Alden Press, Osney Mead, Oxford.

# ACKNOWLEDGMENTS

## A Door in the Hive

Grateful acknowledgement is made to the editors and publishers of magazines in which some of the poems in this collection previously appeared: *Abraxas, Agenda* (England), *American Poetry Review, Amicus Journal, The Artists's Magazine, Cloud* (England), *The Earlhamite, Gown* (Northern Ireland), *Green Mountain Review, Kentucky Poetry Review, Prism, Religion & Intellectual Life, Sandscript, Sequoia, Shenandoah, South Coast Poetry Review, The Southern California Anthology* and *Tampa Review*. One poem also appeared in *Hill Field: Poems and Memoirs for John Montague* (Coffee House Press).

AUTHOR'S NOTE: I would like to thank Nell Blaine for the generous loan of her house in Austria where some of these poems were written; Barbara Hyams for reading Rilke with me (in connection with the Rilke variations in *Breathing the Water* as well as the two in this volume); David Shaddock for advice and response; Yarrow Cleaves for response and typing. Additionally, I owe a retrospective debt of gratitude, in regard to earlier books, to Carlene Carrasco Laughlin, Phyllis Kutt and Steven Blevins.

# Evening Train

Grateful acknowledgement is made to the editors and publishers of magazines in which some of the poems in this collection first appeared: *American Poetry Review, Am Here Forum, Amicus Journal, Aril/Cross Currents, Café Review, Cantilevers, The Catholic Worker, Common Knowledge, In Context, Mississippi Valley Review, New American Writing, Northlight* (Scotland), *Private, Range, Seneca Quarterly, Sojourner, Storm Warning, Verve* and *Zyzzyva.* Some also appeared in the anthologies *After the Storm* and *The WPFW Poetry Anthology.* The poems in Section I, *Lake Mountain Moon,* were published in a limited edition by Tangram Press, which also, separately, published as a limited edition chapbook the suite of poems *Embracing the Multipede.*

AUTHOR'S NOTE: A number of these poems were written at the Rockefeller Foundation's Villa Serbelloni, at Bellagio, Lake Como. I shall always recall my five weeks there with joy and gratitude. The *Two Magnets'* section of this book is dedicated to the memory of Roberto Celli the then director, and to Gianna Celli.

# CONTENTS

## A Door in the Hive

## Evening Train

# A DOOR IN THE HIVE

**I**

## To Rilke

Once, in dream,
                  the boat
pushed off from the shore.
You at the prow were the man –
all voice, though silent – who bound
rowers and voyagers to the needful journey,
the veiled distance, imperative mystery.

All the crouched effort,
        creak of oarlocks, odor of sweat,
        sound of waters
          running against us
was transcended: your gaze
held as we crossed. Its dragonfly blue
restored to us
             a shimmering destination.

I had not read yet of your Nile journey,
the enabling voice
drawing that boat upstream in your parable.
Strange that I knew
your silence was just such a song.

# To R.D., March 4th 1988

You were my mentor. Without knowing it,
I outgrew the need for a mentor.
Without knowing it, you resented that,
and attacked me. I bitterly resented
the attack, and without knowing it
freed myself to move forward
without a mentor. Love and long friendship
corroded, shrank, and vanished from sight
into some underlayer of being.
The years rose and fell, rose and fell,
and the news of your death after years of illness
was a fact without resonance for me,
I had lost you long before, and mourned you,
and put you away like a folded cloth
put away in a drawer. But today I woke
while it was dark, from a dream
that brought you live into my life:
I was in a church, near the Lady Chapel
at the head of the 'west aisle'. Hearing a step
I turned: you were about to enter
the row behind me, but our eyes met
and you smiled at me, your unfocussed eyes
focussing in that smile to renew
all the reality our foolish pride extinguished.
You moved past me then, and as you sat down
beside me, I put a welcoming hand
over yours, and your hand was warm.
I had no need
for a mentor, nor you to be one;
but I was once more
your chosen sister, and you
my chosen brother.
We heard strong harmonies rise and begin to fill
the arching stone,
sounds that had risen here through centuries.

## Intimation

I am impatient with these branches, this light.
The sky, however blue, intrudes.
Because I've begun to see
there is something else I must do,
I can't quite catch the rhythm
of days I moved well to in other winters.
The steeple tree
was cut down, the one that daybreak
used to gild – that fervor of birds and cherubim
subdued. Drought has dulled
many a green blade.
                                    Because
I know a different need has begun
to cast its lines out from me into
a place unknown, I reach
for a silence almost present,
elusive among my heartbeats.

## A Traveler

If it's chariots or sandals,
I'll take sandals.
I like the high prow of the chariot,
the daredevil speed, the wind
a quick tune you can't
quite catch
        but I want to go
a long way
and I want to follow
paths where wheels deadlock.
              And I don't want always
to be among gear and horses,
      blood, foam, dust. I'd like
to wean myself from their strange allure.
I'll chance
the pilgrim sandals.

# Entering Another Chapter

The nights pass, sleep and dreams, the ship rolling and creaking;
and days, clouds rolling soundlessly, creak of seabirds' wings
veering, battling headwinds. Nights, days, out on the main,
passage of years, decades, no landfall fragrance, peppery breeze.
Then a morning comes, this one, of light different
                                        as light in childhood
            when we opened our eyes to an altered ceiling,
            customary shadows absent,
            tenor of morning changed – afraid for a moment,
            then we knew, and jumped out of bed to look,
                  and yes, the mystery
            was indeed the mystery of snowfall.


                  Today, awakening shows a color of ocean
unrecognized. And there are islands. Birds of new species
                                    follow the wake.
The sky too is a sky not witnessed before, its hue
not imagined. Coastal villages, mountain contours almost
                              remembered – yet this
is not any place from which we left, some cognate rather. Travelers
not noticed before stand at the rail beside us. No sense of arrival;
a sense of approach. Some meet our eyes, we begin to speak, to hear
how their story – the long land journey, the port, delays,
                                          embarkation,
      storms, doldrums, then the seductive furrowing through time,
                                    anything else
      receding, paling, fuzzy and then forgotten,
      only the sea present and real, and the ship nosing its way
under moon and sun –
                  was our own story.

# For Instance

Often, it's nowhere special: maybe
a train rattling not fast or slow
from Melbourne to Sydney, and the light's fading,
we've passed that wide river remembered
from a tale about boyhood and fatal love, written
in vodka prose, clear and burning –
the light's fading and then
beside the tracks this particular
straggle of eucalypts, an inconsequential
bit of a wood, a coppice, looks your way,
not at you, through you, through the train,
over it – gazes with branches and rags of bark
to something beyond your passing. It's not,
this shred of seeing, more beautiful
than a million others, less so than many;
you have no past here, no memories,
and you'll never set foot among these shadowy
tentative presences. Perhaps when you've left this continent
you'll never return; but it stays with you:
years later, whenever
its blurry image flicks on in your head,
it wrenches from you the old cry:
O Earth, belovéd Earth!
                              – like many another faint
constellation of landscape does, or fragment
of lichened stone, or some old shed
where you took refuge once from pelting rain
in Essex, leaning on wheel or shafts
of a dusty cart, and came out when you heard
a blackbird return to song though the rain
was not quite over; and, as you thought there'd be,
there was, in the dark quarter where frowning clouds
were still clustered, a hesitant trace
of rainbow; and across from that the expected
gleam of East Anglian afternoon light, and leaves
dripping and shining. Puddles, and the roadside weeds
washed of their dust. Earth,
that inward cry again –
*Erde, du liebe...*

# The Blind Man's House at the Edge of the Cliff

At the jutting rim of the land he lives,
but not from ignorance,
not from despair.
He knows one extra step from his seaward
wide-open door would be
a step into salt air,
and he has no longing to shatter himself
far below, where the breakers
grind granite to sand.
No, he has chosen a life
pitched at the brink, a nest on the swaying
tip of a branch, for good reason:

dazzling within his darkness
is the elusive deep horizon. Here
nothing intrudes, palpable shade,
between his eager
inward gaze
and the vast enigma.
If he could fly he would drift forever
into that veil, soft and receding.

He knows that if he could see
he would be no wiser.
High on the windy cliff he breathes
face to face with desire.

**II**

# Distanced

*If one's fate is to survive only sorrow,*
*one has no right to the name survivor.*

Shepherds in summer pastures
watched the invaders, a rectangular wave,
advance on the city far below. Smoke,
and towers falling. A straggling river
pouring from breached walls.
This high, no noises reached them.

They marvelled, they sorrowed.
Each had wished some day
to see for himself the city's
alien glories; all felt pity and dread.
They knew the river
was people fleeing.

But they could see no faces,
and no blood.

# Land of Death Squads

The vultures thrive,
clustered in lofty blue above
refuse-dumps where humans too
search for food, dreading
what else may be found.
Noble their wingspread,
hideous their descent
to those who know
what they may feast on:
sons, daughters.
And meanwhile,
the quetzal, bird of life, gleaming
green, glittering red, is driven
always further, higher,
into remote
ever-dwindling forests.

# El Salvador: Requiem and Invocation
*(A Libretto)*


Not long after the murders of Archbishop Oscar Romero and of the three American nuns and a lay sister in El Salvador, I was asked by the composer Newell Hendricks to provide a text for him to work with in composing an oratorio. I suggested El Salvador as a theme, and these martyrdoms as a focus; and he was receptive to the idea. Drawing on my knowledge of Mexico and some research into Salvadoran history, I also obtained copies of letters written home by the four assassinated women as well as excerpts from Archbishop Romero's homilies. What I then attempted to write was not conceived as a poem so much as a working text for the composer – that is to say, I wanted to avoid certain nuances of rhythm and pitch in my words in order to produce something deliberately incomplete, something broadly sketched which would call precisely for that development the still unwritten music would give it. Please see the note on pages 214-15 for further details of the piece's sources and development. – D.L.


*\*Actual quotations from eyewitness accounts*

# El Salvador: Requiem and Invocation

CHORUS *(Words of Terror and Violence)*

Blood Rape Kill Mutilate Death-squad Massacre
Torture Acid Order National Guard Thirst Pain
Crying Screaming Bloated Naked Helicopter
Slaughter Shoot Machine-gunned Beaten Vomit
Slash Burning Slit Bullhorns Sprayed Blinded
Bullets Machete Wounds Smash

*(Phrases of Terror and Violence)*
They cut off their heads They cut off their hands
They cut off their balls They cut off their breasts
Chopped up his face Hacking dead meat
The crops are burning 'Mama, they're burning
my dress!' 'The empire of hell' 'Hit them – hit them
again' 'We've hit them already – they'll
just die – leave them'
'I had a terrible thirst' 'The water was full of blood'
'Blood of my children' 'I kept drinking, drinking
the water. It was full of blood.'
'Kill the survivors' 'Tie their thumbs behind their
backs.' 'Acid is thrown in their faces.'
'We have seen too much, too many dead.'*
The air is black with smoke. No one is safe.

VOICE OF QUESTIONER

O Mayan land! El Salvador!
What brought you to this time
of horror? Long ago
            it was not so –

CHORUS

Long ago
it was not so,
the land was generous,
the people lived at peace.
The land and people
were one, and lived
at peace:

NARRATOR

Long ago, in the far millenia,
already the Mayan folk were tending
pumpkins & chili,
corn and beans:
the earth was bountiful,
it gave freely:

CHORUS

avocado, guava, papaya,
blackberry, elderberry,
tomato and calabash,
*sapote, nopale* –

NARRATOR

The people lived
with reverence, knowing
the daily mystery:
earth, sky, plants, men & women,
inseparable,
a single mystery:

The hoe, the digging stick,
were tools of a sacrament.
Prayers rose night & day
from the deep valleys,
from the lowlands,
from the mountainslopes
in the shimmering dust of months that are hot & dry,
in the great rains of summer
when thunder cracks its whip.
They knew the cycle, the rituals:
earth & sky,
fruits, animals,
humans:

PRAYER *(Chorus)*

'O God,
Lord of the hills & valleys,
I am beneath thy feet,
beneath thy hands –

O God, my grandfather,
O God, my grandmother,
            God of the hills,
            God of the valleys,
my holy God:
                I make to you my offering
                with all my soul.
Be patient with me in what I am doing.

It is needful that you give me
all I am going to sow here,
here where I have my work,
my cornfield;
watch it for me,
guard my field for me, my *milpa*,
let it be safe,
from the time of sowing
to the time of harvest.'*

NARRATOR

And once a year
for five days there was silence –

CHORUS

Once a year
hide
in darkness
under roofs,
indoors –
do nothing,
don't eat
don't make love
don't speak,
hide
in darkness

the gods
are not here
not there
we know
nothing

* *Kakehi Indian prayer*

we must
be still
be patient
in limbo,
holding our breath,
for then,
after silence
life will
continue,
earth & sky,
fruit and folk...

NARRATOR

And life continued, slow, long ago, the rhythms
of that slow dance, grandmother earth,
grandfather sky, their children & children's children.

VOICE OF QUESTIONER

And then, and then?
   How did the horror begin?
Was it a thunderclap? Did men
blaspheme?

NARRATOR

Not with a thunderclap,
but yes,
with blasphemy:
but not the Maya blasphemed:
men from a far place,
a few, & a few, then more,
more – yet still
only a few, but powerful
with alien power –
came seeking gold,
        seeking wealth,
        denying
        the mystery of the land,
        the sacred harmony,
        breaking the rhythm
        taking the earth unto themselves
        to use it –

NARRATOR

But now among those
who long ago had come with the conquerors
bearing aloft the image of a God they said was good,
in whose name they and
the conquerors, soldiers of fortune,
took power,
             took power and gave to the people
not God's good but evil;
who crushed the people as they
crushed the old gods,
who came as priests of conquest –
now among these were heard
       new voices
       voices of mercy
       voices of pity
       voices of love for the poor;

CHORUS

and now
the nuns, priests, bishops,
not only spoke but listened,

and listening gave
the great gift of attention,
and fed the hungry
not with scraps and crumbs of
    uncharitable charity
but with respect,
calling for justice.

NARRATOR

And strongest among them, a voice leading the chorus,
Oscar Romero, the Arch-
bishop, 'prince of the church', whose riches
were faith, hope, and love,
who, day by day,
       week by week,
gathered testimony of terror,
of 'the insulted and injured' –

ROMERO

'the clamor of the people, the aching
of so much crime, the ignominy
of so much violence' †

NARRATOR

– and broadcast it, Sunday by Sunday

CHORUS

– that no general
          no member of the Junta
          no National Guardsman
          no business tycoon
could claim innocence, ignorance;
no side of the great multifaceted
crime of oppression
would go undenounced.

NARRATOR

And each week he read
the roll of names of the newly dead –
of the men, women, and children
abducted, tortured, killed, disappeared
that week.
          He was Archbishop:
the junta's anger
smouldered.

ROMERO

ANTONIO FLORES
SANDRA MARITZA GALICIA
EVE CATALINA HERNANDEZ
DENIS ORLANDO GALLARDO
BORIS NAPOLEAN MARTINEZ
JAIME ANDRES LOPEZ CASTELLON
SONIA ELIZABETH MEJIA
JUAN RAMON PEREZ SANDOVAL
BLANCA ESTELA CONTRERAS
RAMIRO ENRIQUEZ

† *This and all subsequent quotations by Romero
are taken from his public statements*

36

RAUL OMAR ROSALES CAMPOS
RICARDO ERNESTO ORELLANA
EDWIN CHAVEZ
ADILSON MELENDEZ SOMOZA
DEMESIO ZETINO RODRIQUEZ
LORI ROBERTO ORELLANA SANCHES
JOSE ROBERTO PONCE VELASQUEZ
JOSE GUIERMO CARPIO
MARCO ANTONIO CARCAMO DONA
ANTONIO DUBON SANCHEZ
ARISTIDES WILFREDO CASTILLO
EFRIAN MENJIVAR
YURI ELMER ARIA NOVOA
CLAUDIA INES CUELLAR COTO
JUAN MANUEL RODRIQUEZ
ADOLFO BERNAL MEJIA
MARIA CRISTINA JUAREZ
MARIA ALICIA PEREZ
ROSA MARGARITA JOAQUIN
LUIS ALBERTO DIAZ SERRANO
LUZ VASQUEZ MEJIA RIVERA
IVAN CUELLAS GIRON
CARLOS ARMANDO SERRANO
NAPOLEAN DE MONGE RIVERA
MARIA TERESA MANJIVAR
CARLOS ARMANDO MEDINA
HAYDEE YANIRA RIVERA
GORGE ANDRES CHACON SEQURA
ROXANA QUITANILLA
RENE SANTOS
EDUARDO SANTOS
ELMA MOJICA
SERGIO MOJICA SANTOS
WALTER SANTOS
DELMA SANTOS
MORENA SANTOS
BEATRIZ SANTOS
SONIA MOJICA
TOMMASA SANTOS
HERMINA SANTOS
ERASMO VLADIMIRO SANTOS
VENECIA AND VICTORIA SANTOS
ROSA SANTOS
TERESA SANTOS
ELBA SANTOS
ROSA MOJICA
MARCOS MOJICA SANTOS
HUGO MOJICA SANTOS...*

*Voice continues diminuendo behind chorus*

The pain, the murders,
the hunger, the tortures,
all continued,
and continue still,
and increase –

yet the voices that tell us
our broken bodies are not after all
worthless rubbish, but hold
sparks of the God –
                                these voices
begin to give us our freedom:

HALF CHORUS

Though we have lost
knowledge of old harmonies,
old ways we spoke to the earth,
                    sang to the sky –
though we have lost
the knowledge we had
            of grandfather, grandmother
            god in the ear of corn,
            god in the cocoa-bean,
            god the rain and
            god the sun –

CHORUS

Yet now
our dignity grows in us
once more,
we believe
there is life in our land
to be lived,
that our anguish
moves us onward, forward towards
a time of justice...

NARRATOR

And time was passing,
quickly, quickly,
here in the small land of El Salvador
as in the rest of the troubled globe,
where wars and hunger and fear
convulse and contort
like vast and poisonous clouds
battling in nightmare skies
as the century's last quarter
hurtles toward the unknown –
and into this chaos
    where daily among the people
    priests and nuns risked with the rest
    torture, 'disappearance', mutilation,

CHORUS

FATHER MARCIEL SERRANO
FATHER ERNESTO ABREGO
FATHER RUTILIO GRANDE
SISTER SYLVIA MARIBEL ARRIOLA...*

NARRATOR

and into this chaos arrived four women
out of the north –

CHORUS

– out of that land
whose money and power and weapons
support our oppressors, and teach
the junta's killers
new ways of killing:
four Yanqui nuns –

NARRATOR

– arrived to join
their sisters and serve the people:
Ita, Maura, Jean, Dorothy.

* Chorus continues with additional names

39

**DOROTHY**

'We have come to a land that
is writhing in pain…
Yet a land that's waiting, hoping,
yearning for peace.'*

**MAURA**

'We came in answer
to a call. The need
is overwhelming.'*

**ITA**

'We came to live with the poor.
To be
evangelized by the poor.'*

**JEAN**

'I was a lay missioner.
I came to give
two years of myself.
I was not planning to stay.'*

**ALL FOUR**

'We have come to a land that
is writhing in pain.
Yet a land that's waiting, hoping,
yearning for peace.'*

**NARRATOR**

And Romero spoke to the soldiers,
the National Guard, the police,
                    saying,

**ROMERO**

'Brothers, you belong
to our own people! You kill
your brother peasants!
Stop the killing – for no one
has to comply with immoral orders,
immoral laws.'†

* *These and all subsequent quotations by the four sisters are taken from their letters.*

40

**NARRATOR**

And Romero spoke to the government,
saying,

**ROMERO**

'Reforms mean nothing
when they are bathed
in so much blood.'†

**CHORUS**

We are refugees
in our own country,
herded and huddled
now here, now there –

**SISTERS** *(Singly)*

'We came to bring food and shelter'
'To search for the missing'
'To help in the struggle to break
out of the bonds
    of oppression
    and hunger
    and violence' –

**SISTERS** *(Together)*

'in a land that is writhing in pain,
yearning for peace,'*

**CHORUS** *(Overlap echo effect)*

So much blood
        So much blood

So many deaths
        So many deaths

So much courage
        So much courage

So much endurance
        So much endurance

So much faith
        So much faith

CHORUS

We learned
how the old gods, our grandparents, long betrayed,
unite with the god our martyred friends
brought in their hearts to us: the crucified –
        who refused to be bought,
        who suffered like us,
        who returned from the dead.

SISTERS *(Together)*

'In a land that is writhing in pain,
yearning for peace,'*

to suffer the powerlessness of the poor
and to go beyond it,

to discover,
to discover and to reveal

the power of that powerlessness.

CHORUS *(With irony)*

Powerless, feathers in a whirlpool,
they were killed,
of course. (ECHO: Of course, of course, of course...)

VOICE OF QUESTIONER

O Mayan land! El Salvador!
what brought you to this time
of horror?

NARRATOR

Archbishop Romero gunned down
in the hospice for incurables,
named for Divine Providence:
his killers
chose their moment.
He fell
at the altar, saying
a requiem mass, saying
'Let us unite' –

42

**ROMERO**

'Let us unite in faith and hope
as we pray
for the dead
and for ourselves.'†

**NARRATOR**

A magnum slug,
his heart torn open,
a single shot,
a hired killer,
a distance of 20 meters.

**HALF CHORUS**

His killers
were ironic;
*but in martyrdom*
*is a seed of power!*

**NARRATOR**

The sisters, travelling
on their road of mercy,
were ambushed,
raped,
killed,
flung in a pit.

**HALF CHORUS** *(bitterly ironic)*

Raped, killed, flung in a pit –
the usual way.
The soldiers
had practice.
*But in martyrdom*
*is a seed of power.*

**VOICE OF QUESTIONER**

What do they ask,
the martyrs,
of those who hear them,
who know

the story, the cry,
who know what brought
our land to this grief?
What do their deaths demand?

ROMERO AND FOUR SISTERS

We ask that our story be known
not as the story of Salvador only;
everywhere, greed
exploits the people,
everywhere, greed
gives birth to violence,
everywhere, violence
at last is answered with violence:
    the desperate turn,
convulsed with pain,
to desperate means.

HALF CHORUS

Those who were martyred
bequeathed, a gift to the living,
their vision:
they saw, they told in their lives that violence
is not justice, that merciless justice
is not justice, that mercy
does not bind up
festering wounds,
but scrapes out the poison.

That 'no one has to comply
with immoral laws,'†

that power abused is powerless to crush
the spirit.

HALF CHORUS

Now we still writhe in agony,
violent against
the unceasing violence of greed,
the greed for profit, the greed for power,
the greed of faraway strangers
to hold the world's power in their hands.

44

Desperation
drives us: we take no joy
in bloodshed: our longing,
our longing, our longing,
is for Peace and the works of Peace:

even now in the hidden villages,
in the mountain camps,
schools for the people spring up
like corn in the ancient *milpas* –
play and knowledge for children,
dignity for women, hope for men,
poems and songs of the people:
all of this
is for Peace. For this
our martyrs died.
Their deaths
enjoin upon us, the living,
not to give up the vision
of lives freed from the lead weight
of centuries, clear of the stain
                    of indigo, stench
                    of fermenting sugar,
                    whistle of whiplash,
                    cramps of hunger,
                    ache of lost dignity, loss
                    of the ancient rhythms –
vision of simple peace,
sharing our minds, our labor, our soup,
teaching hope to our children,
putting behind us
the terror of centuries.


CHORUS

Those who were martyred –
Romero,
        Maura,
                Ita,
                    Dorothy,
                            Jean –
and those whose names
are lost along with their bodies –
all the Marias and Juans, the Josés and Pedros,

Elenas and Glorias – they tell us,
                    we in El Salvador, you
our sisters and brothers who know
the story,
all of us, all –
they tell us that horror
won't cease on the earth
till the hungry are fed,

that the fruits of the earth
don't grow that a few may profit,

that injustice here
is one with injustice anywhere,
all of us *are*
our brother's keepers,
members one of another,
responsible, culpable, and –

*able to change.*
This is the knowledge
that grows in power
out of the seeds of their martyrdom.

ROMERO AND FOUR SISTERS

Let us unite
in faith and hope
as we pray
for the dead
and for ourselves.

ALL

Let us unite
in faith and hope
as we pray:
as we pray for the dead
in faith and hope:
in faith and hope
as we pray:

as we pray for ourselves
for faith
as we pray
for hope.

46

# The Book Without Words
*(from a painting by Anselm Kiefer)*


The gray waves gnash
their teeth of foam.

Behind this verge,
the barren plain,
seamed, fissured.

Ahead, limitless ocean.
The sky's low ceiling
bears down upon it,
dark and darkening.

Here at the end of land
(not earth but cinders)

was to have been given
the ultimate direction.
The sea-voyage was to begin.

And indeed the book
is here, a huge volume,
open and upright –
it levitates, close to the hiss of spume,

immutable, desolate, cast
in lead. Wordless.
If with great force its pages
were made to turn,
they would knock, unresonant,

one on another,
void upon void.
You have come to the shore.
There are no instructions.

# Variation on a Theme by Rilke
*(The Book of Hours, Poem 8)*

Soon, the end of a century. Is the great scroll
being shaken, the scroll
inscribed by God and daubed with our lives' graffiti,

to raise this wind that churns
the sleep of listeners?
What holds aloft
that banner, that undeciphered legend?

Familiar powers extend towards it
their fingers of bone –
it lifts
      beyond reach,
an elusive kite.

And the wind
rises and rises, the powers
exchange dark looks, the sleepers
watch and listen.

                       Is there more parchment
wound, still, on the heavy spindle?
If, when the scroll unfurls, it reveals
a pallid, empty field,
               what shall be written there?
Where, if we discover the runes continue,
shall we seek out
         their hierophant?

# In California: Morning, Evening, Late January

Pale, then enkindled,
light
advancing,
emblazoning
summits of palm and pine,

the dew
lingering,
scripture of
scintillas.

Soon the roar
of mowers
cropping the already short
grass of lawns,

men with long-nozzled
cylinders of pesticide
poking at weeds,
at moss in cracks of cement,

and louder roar
of helicopters off to spray
vineyards where *braceros* try
to hold their breath,

and in the distance, bulldozers, excavators,
babel of destructive construction.

Banded by deep
oakshadow, airy
shadow of eucalyptus,

miner's lettuce,
tender, untasted,

and other grass, unmown,
luxuriant,
no green more brilliant.

Fragile paradise.

* * * *

At day's end the whole sky,
vast, unstinting, flooded with transparent
mauve,
tint of wisteria,
cloudless
over the malls, the industrial parks,
the homes with the lights going on,
the homeless arranging their bundles.

* * * *

Who can utter
the poignance of all that is constantly
threatened, invaded, expended

and constantly
nevertheless
persists in beauty,

tranquil as this young moon
just risen and slowly
drinking light
from the vanished sun.

Who can utter
the praise of such generosity
or the shame?

## Those Who Want Out

In their homes, much glass and steel. Their cars
are fast – walking's for children, except in rooms.
When they take longer trips, they think with contempt
of the jet's archaic slowness. Monastic
in dedication to work, they apply honed skills,
impatient of less than perfection. They sleep by day
when the bustle of lives might disturb their research,
and labor beneath fluorescent light in controlled environments
fitting their needs, as the dialects
in which they converse, with each other or with
the machines (which are not called machines)
are controlled and fitting. The air they breathe
is conditioned. Coffee and coke keep them alert.
But no one can say they don't dream,
that they have no vision. Their vision
consumes them, they think all the time
of the city in space, they long for the permanent colony,
not just a lab up there, the whole works,
malls, raquet courts, hot tubs, state-of-the-art
ski machines, entertainment...Imagine it, they think,
way out there, outside of 'nature', unhampered,
a place contrived by man, supreme
triumph of reason. They know it will happen.
*They do not love the earth.*

# Two Threnodies and a Psalm

### I

It is not approaching.
It has arrived.
We are not circumventing it.

It is happening.
It is happening now.
We are not preventing it.
We are within it.

\*

The sound of its happening
is splitting other ears.
The sight of its happening
is searing other eyes.
The grip of its happening
is strangling other throats.

\*

Without intermission it spins,
without cessation we circle its edge
as leaf or crumb will float circling
a long time at the outer rim
before centripetal force
tugs it down.

### II

The body being savaged
is alive.
It is our own.

While the eagle-vulture
tears the earth's liver,
while the heart-worm burrows
into earth's heart,

we are distant from what devours us
only as far as our extremities are from our minds,
which is no great distance.

        \*

Extremities, we are in
unacknowledged *extremis*.
We feel only
a chill as the pulse of life
recedes.

We don't beat off the devouring beak,
the talons. We don't dig out what burrows
into our core. *It is not
our heart, we think* (but do not say).
*It is the world's, poor world, but I
am other.*

### III

Our clear water
one with the infested water
      women walk miles to
      each day they live.
One with the rivers tainted with detritus
            of our ambitions,
and with the dishonored ocean.
Our unbroken skin
one with the ripped skin of the tortured,
      the shot-down, bombed, napalmed,
      the burned alive.
One with the sore and filthy skin of the destitute.

        \*

We utter the words
*we are one*
but their truth
is not real to us.

Spirit, waken
our understanding.

Out of the stasis
in which we perish,
the sullen immobility
to which the lead weight of our disbelief
condemns us,
only your rushing wind
can lift us.

*

Our flesh and theirs
one with the flesh of fruit and tree.

Our blood
one with the blood of whale and sparrow.

Our bones
ash and cinder of star-fire.

Our being
tinder for primal light.

*

Lift us, Spirit, impel
our rising
into that knowledge.

Make truth real to us,
flame on our lips.

Lift us to seize the present,
wrench it
out of its downspin.

# Kin and Kin

*(for William Everson)*


Perhaps Jeffers was right, our species
best unborn, and once born
better soon gone, a criminal kind,
the planet's nightmare. Our going
would leave no hauntings at all, unless
to the last of those we've tamed or caged;
after those, a world
fierce in the hunt but free from malice
and free from remembrance.

Yet there have been the wise, the earthen elders
humble before the grass.
When from the torturers, picking their teeth
after a full meal, relaxed
after a full day of their routine job, we turn
to regard such others, remote as they are, yet kin –
as wheat and weed are kin, each
having root, stem, seed – or when
we hear some note of kindness
innocent of its own courage amid
the clamor of lies, it seems after all

there might be open to us, even now,
a chance to evolve, a swerve we could take,
a destiny still held out (if we would look)
in the Spirit's palm.

# On the Mystery of the Incarnation

It's when we face for a moment
the worst our kind can do, and shudder to know
the taint in our own selves, that awe
cracks the mind's shell and enters the heart:
not to a flower, not to a dolphin,
to no innocent form
but to this creature vainly sure
it and no other is god-like, God
(out of compassion for our ugly
failure to evolve) entrusts,
as guest, as brother,
the Word.

**III**

# Where Is the Angel?

Where is the angel for me to wrestle?
No driving snow in the glass bubble,
but mild September.

Outside, the stark shadows
menace, and fling their huge arms about
unheard. I breathe

a tepid air, the blur
of asters, of brown fern and gold-dust
seems to murmur,

and that's what I hear, only that.
Such clear walls of curved glass:
I see the violent gesticulations

and feel – no, not nothing. But in this
gentle haze, nothing commensurate.
It is pleasant in here. History

mouths, volume turned off. A band of iron,
like they put round a split tree,
circles my heart. In here

it is pleasant, but when I open
my mouth to speak, I too
am soundless. Where is the angel

to wrestle with me and wound
not my thigh but my throat,
so curses and blessings flow storming out
and the glass shatters, and the iron sunders?

## Soutine
*(Two Paintings)*


As if the forks themselves
were avid for the fish,
dead scrawny fish
on dead-white plate.
As if the red steps
were clutching the hill,
famished,
crawling toward the summit.
O desperate things,
living lives unheeded,
disbelieved
by those who made them!
O grey void, usurping
the abandoned cup's
parched hollow!

And houses lean, wavering,
to watch if the steps will ever
arrive, and what could there be,
up there,
to fulfil desire?

# The Love of Morning

It is hard sometimes to drag ourselves
back to the love of morning
after we've lain in the dark crying out
O God, save us from the horror...

God has saved the world one more day
even with its leaden burden of human evil;
we wake to birdsong.
And if sunlight's gossamer lifts in its net
the weight of all that is solid,
our hearts, too, are lifted,
swung like laughing infants;

but on gray mornings,
all incident – our own hunger,
the dear tasks of continuance,
the footsteps before us in the earth's
belovéd dust, leading the way – all,
is hard to love again
for we resent a summons
that disregards our sloth, and this
calls us, calls us.

# The Winter Stars

Last night the stars had a brilliance more insistent
than I'd seen for months. The sword of Orion poised
ready to strike – one of the few constellations I know.
      Once for a short while
I lived by a lake. Each day a gentle man
who knew much about poetry, much about William Blake,
but spoke with a painful stutter, brought to my door
food, messages, friendship;
sometimes his two young sons came with him,
one of them just recovered from dangerous illness.
It snowed while I was there
and I took a photo that caught
the large loose flakes descending
among awestruck tall and straight young trees.
But mostly that winter it was so warm
by noon you could sit outdoors
and the Canada geese had halted
on their way south, encamped, like me, on the shore.
Heading out each day in captained hundreds
to forage, they returned at dusk,
troop by troop, and barked the day's luck to each other,
a multifold, intimate tribal lay...
In the cottage, where all was old, delicate, friendly,
I wrote a poem to the antique clock that for years
had peacefully kept its own time.
Before sleep I would stop outdoors:
the lake silent, no wind in the trees,
the throng of geese at rest, but always
a few of them stirring;
and the winter stars.
      Later the man and one of his sons
(I never found out which one, whether the boy
death had already fingered and left,
or the one more robust)
were killed by a drunken driver.
The wife and the lonely brother
moved away. 'Eating the bread of bitterness' was the phrase
that came to my mind. There had been
much love and kindness among those four.

There are clusters, constellations,
one can perceive as grouped
but which suggest no figure of myth,
no meaning. The stars which give
a clue to the pattern
are too many light-years away, perhaps,
for our eyes, or our telescopes,
or even our inner vision.
Those we perceive can seem
to threaten us or implore, so insistently
their remote beauty glitters upon us,
and with such silence.

# Two Mountains

*To perceive the aura of an object,*
*we look at means to invest it with*
*the ability to look at us in return.*
WALTER BENJAMIN

For a month (a minute)
I lived in sight of two mountains.
One was a sheer bastion
of pale rock. 'A rockface,' one says,
without thought of features, expression –
it's an abstract term.
        But one says, too,
'a stony-faced man,' or 'she maintained
a stony silence.' This mountain,
had it had eyes, would have looked always
past one or through one; its mouth,
if it had one, would purse thin lips,
implacable, ceding nothing, nothing at all.

The other mountain gave forth
a quite different silence.
Even (beyond my range of hearing)
it may have been singing.
Ravines, forests, bare rock that peaked, off-center
in a sharp and elegant cone or horn, had an air
of pleasure, pleasure in being.
At this one I looked and looked
but could devise
no ruse to coax it to meet my gaze.
I had to accept its complete indifference,
my own complete insignificance,
my self
        unknowable to the mountain
as a single needle of spruce or fir
on its distant slopes, to me.

## In Tonga

the sacred bats
hang in their chosen grove,
      sinister old dustbags,
      charcoal gray,
doze upside down,
      alien, innocent.
Restless, like seals on a rock,
they nudge one another,
they slip off into air to circle
           the trees and
return, squeaking their utterance,
a fluttering language, and others, disturbed,
squeak in reproof.
           All day in the heat
they wait
for dusk and the high
invisible orchards.

If they could think
it would not be of us.

# A Sound

### 1

An unexplained sound, today,
in the early sunlight
and no wind stirring the leaves,
of something breathing
                    surrounds the house,
quiet, regular, as of someone
peacefully dreaming; something close,
yet not located: one can't say,
'it comes from beneath the southwest window,'
for, go to the north window,
it breathes there too.

### 2

                    They say that once,
and in living memory, orchards of apricot,
nectarine, peach, filled this valley.
In spring it drifted in ruffles
of lacy white, of lacy pink.
And before that time, for centuries
months would go by each year when no human gaze
witnessed the changes here. Forest or grassland,
green to tawny and slowly
back to green as the seasons
paced in their circle-dance. The oaks
were thick on the hills.

### 3

Whatever was breathing nearby,
early today, I can't hear
now that the sun is high.
It woke, perhaps, and softly
removed itself. Or maybe
it turned in its sleep,
lowered itself to new depths of dream,
soundless. I think I shall hear it
breathing some day again. Or if I'm gone,
no matter – I think the sound
will recur. It need not be heard.

# Envy

The bare trees
have made up their seed bundles.
They are ready now.
The warm brown light
pauses briefly, shrugs and moves on.
They are ready now
to play dead for a while.
I, human, have not as yet devised
how to obtain
such privilege.
Their Spring will find them rested.
I and my kind
battle a wakeful way
to ours.

# Complicity

On the young tree's highest twig,
a dark leaf, dry, solitary, left over
from winter, among the small new buds.
But it turns its head!
                    It's a hummingbird,
tranquil, at rest, taking time off
from the hummingbird world of swift intensities –
yet no less attentive. Taking
a long and secret look at the day,
like a child whose hiding-place
has not been discovered, who hasn't even
been missed. No hue and cry.
                              I saw
a leaf: I shall not betray you.

# Flickering Mind

Lord, not you,
it is I who am absent.
At first
belief was a joy I kept in secret,
stealing alone
into sacred places:
a quick glance, and away – and back,
circling.
I have long since uttered your name
but now
I elude your presence.
I stop
to think about you, and my mind
at once
like a minnow darts away,
darts
into the shadows, into gleams that fret
unceasing over
the river's purling and passing.
Not for one second
will my self hold still, but wanders
anywhere,
everywhere it can turn. Not you,
it is I am absent.
You are the stream, the fish, the light,
the pulsing shadow,
you the unchanging presence, in whom all
moves and changes.
How can I focus my flickering, perceive
at the fountain's heart
the sapphire I know is there?

# A Stone from Iona

Men who planned to be hermits, hoped to be saints, arrived
in a round boat of wicker and skin at a pebbled cove.
Behind them, dangerous leagues of mist and wave
and behind those, a land belov'd and renounced. Before them,
beyond the slope of stones and the massed green
spears of iris, waited the island, habitation of birds
and of spirits unknown, dwellers in mounds and hummocks.

Under Columba's saltwashed toes, then jostled beneath
sacks of provisions, and briefly hidden under the coracle
brothers lifted to safety above the tideline, lay
this stone, almost a seabird's egg in form, in color
a white that, placed upon white, is revealed as pearl grey.
Now worn down by fourteen more centuries, its lustre
perhaps has increased, as if moonlight, patiently
blanching and stroking, had aided weather and water
in its perfecting.
                              Hold the stone in your palm:
it fills it, warm when your need is for warmth,
cool when you seek the touch of shadow. Its weight
gives pleasure. One stone is not like another.

## The Sculptor
*(Homage to Chillida)*


A man who lives with his shadow
on equal terms,

who learns from his shadow the arcane power
of right-angles:
>                ascension and lever,
>                taproot and flower.

A man who transmutes
mass into fire: from red, gold; from gold, white –
>                iron accepting rapture, moving,
>                returning satisfied to its purpled
>                black density, secretly curved.

Who permits stone
to acknowledge the inward void it compresses.

And to the impatient sea, the sea who knows everything,
gives immutable combs for its rushing tresses,

new gestures lifted
to the wind, new spouts
for the water curled by the wind
to pour itself into and leap from, shouting.

# Early

From behind the hill,
flowing through somber
palm, eucalyptus, web
of oakboughs, rises
light so pale a gold
it bathes in silver
the cool and still
air a single bird
stirs with tentative song.

## The Braiding

The way the willow-bark
braids its furrows
is answered by the willow-branches
swaying their green leaf-weavings
over the river shallows,
assenting, affirming.

## At One

The mountain's spine, the cow's ridge,
the saddle dip,
                   high flanks,
spur of ranged
spruce, tail
to brush at flies, valley air
between them, and
                   nothing else.

# Web

Intricate and untraceable
weaving and interweaving,
dark strand with light:

designed, beyond
all spiderly contrivance,
to link, not to entrap:

elation, grief, joy, contrition, entwined;
shaking, changing,
                    forever
                        forming,
                            transforming:

*all praise,*
        *all praise to the*
                *great web.*

## The Sorcerer

Blue-eyed Oberon prances
for joy in winter dusk,
the stars
are sparks from his deep, cold fur.
Motifs of Samoyed song
float forth from black lips.
                    For my part
I want the indoors, hot tea,
cherry jam. Yet I linger:
everything
instant by instant
intensifies,
dusk darker, stars wilder.
                 And Oberon,
strange-eyed Oberon,
meets my gaze in stillness
and holds it
          before
he dances homeward,
dog and shaman.

## Flying High

So much is happening above the overcast!
Cloud poets, metaphysicians, essayists,
fabulists of the troposphere,
all at work, the material
their own metamorphic substance:
here a frank exposition, suds you could wash your clothes in,
there an abstract brocade that loops and swivels
in rivers of air. We glide low
across a forest, league on league
of trees in abundant leaf,
but white, silver-white, smudged with blue, tinged
with pink, like peonies – an entire summer
conjured in milky vapor, smoke of alabaster, slivers
of pearl. League on league
to a horizon more remote
than earth's horizons. Fading now,
curling, unfolding, imperceptibly flowing,
the blush paling. Dense thickets migrate
slowly across the fertile cloud-savannah, browsing.
And far aloft, in the sky's own sky, reclined,
the shepherd moon, propped on one elbow, watches
the flocks of drowsy cloud-lambs nibble their way out of being:
for darkness, even here, is gathering; the lunar gaze
dilates and begins to gleam,
while our enormous air-bus, throbbing west and south,
seems to tarry, fleck of metallic dust,
in this firmament where dreamy energies
sculpt themselves and winnow
epic epiphanies.

## Praise of a Palmtree

Tufts of brassy henna in the palm's
shaggy topknot – O Palm,
I like it, I like it!
                    And the dingy underlayer,
bedraggled skirt, tattered collar
around your furrowed neck, or is it your body,
that stout column?
                    You stay awake
all night every night
and tonight will be full moon. It's March,
and the ground beneath you
crunches under bicycle tires
where you littered it with your fruit,
those shiny brown things – I must take
a nutcracker to one some day, are they edible?
You let them fall
like a kid in the movies dropping a trail of popcorn.
                    Are you asleep up there,
your tousled green uncombed,
sunning yourself? Your way of paying
no attention, feline, and yet
strutting your crazy finery fit to kill,
I like it, I like it.

## August Houseplant

Is there someone,
                    an intruder,
in my back yard? That slight
scraping sound again – only a cat
maybe?
            – I look from the screendoor:
Ah! It's you, dear leaves,
only you, big, wildly branching leaves
of the philodendron,
summering on the deck,
            touching the floor of it, feeling
            the chair,
                        exploring.
As if you knew
                    fall is coming, you seem to desire
        everything that surrounds you,
                    all of air,
                        all of light,
                            all of shade.
How am I going to carry you in,
when it gets cold?
                        It's not
that I can't manage the weight
of your pot of earth, though it's heavy.
It's those long, ever-longer, reaching arms
that don't fit through the door.
                    And when you're manoeuvered in,
how small the room will become;
        how can I set you
                    where your green questions
won't lean over human shoulders, obscuring
books and notepads, interrupting
trains of thought
                    to enquire,
                    mutely patient,
                    about the walls?

# Rearrangement

Old chimney bricks, dull red,
sometimes charred in a manner resembling
the way some painters shade
tone into deeper tone:
I'm using them to mark
a new-dug bed where yesterday,
weak and uncertain-looking,
small annuals were planted. Things
get moved around, purposes
redefined.
The bricks aren't beautiful – but time
may change them, after their years
of heat and smoke. Time in the rain.

# A Surrogate

The nearest leaves, outside the glass,
let through no light

but those beyond them
are so filled with ecstatic green
it brims over, cloud of brilliance,
            hovering ocean, glowing
      behind the dark others

that sway, ornate, specific, lobed, opaque,
each with its destiny,

defined upon that dazzling screen
which seems the very source,
for this hour,
of illumination.

**V**

# On the Parables of the Mustard Seed

*(Matthew 17.20, Mark 4.30-32, Luke 13.18-19)*


Who ever saw the mustard-plant,
wayside weed or tended crop,
grow tall as a shrub, let alone a tree, a treeful
of shade and nests and songs?
Acres of yellow,
not a bird of the air in sight.

No, He who knew
the west wind brings
the rain, the south wind
thunder, who walked the field-paths
running His hand along wheatstems to glean
those intimate milky kernels, good
to break on the tongue,

was talking of miracle, the seed
within us, so small
we take it for worthless, a mustard-seed, dust,
nothing.
          Glib generations mistake
the metaphor, not looking at fields and trees,
not noticing paradox. Mountains
remain unmoved.

Faith is rare, He must have been saying,
prodigious, unique –
one infinitesimal grain divided
like loaves and fishes,

*as if* from a mustard-seed
a great shade-tree grew. That rare,
that strange: the kingdom
                a tree. The soul
a bird. A great concourse of birds
at home there, wings among yellow flowers.
The waiting
kingdom of faith, the seed
waiting to be sown.

# The Life of Art

The borderland – that's where, if one knew how,
one would establish residence. That watershed,
that spine, that looking-glass...I mean the edge
between impasto surface, burnt sienna, thick,
      striate, gleaming – swathes and windrows
      of carnal paint –
      or, canvas barely stained,
      where warp and weft peer through,

and fictive truth: a room, a vase, an open door
giving upon the clouds.

A step back, and you have
the likeness, its own world. Step to the wall again,
and you're so near the paint you could lick it,
you breathe its ghostly turpentine.
                        But there's an interface,
immeasurable, elusive – an equilibrium
just attainable, sometimes, when the attention's rightly poised,
where you are opulently received
by the bravura gestures hand and brush
proffer (as if a courtier twirled
a feathered velvet hat to bow you in)
and yet, without losing sight of one stroke,
             one scrape of the knife,
you are drawn through *into* that room, into
its air and temperature.

Couldn't one learn to maintain
that exquisite balance more than a second?
                    (One sees even
the pencilled understrokes, and shivers
in pleasure – *and* one's fingertips
touch the carpet's nubs of wool, the cold fruit in a bowl:
one almost sees
what lies beyond the window, past the frame, beyond...

# Annunciation

*Hail, space for the uncontained God*
    – From the Agathistos Hymn, Greece, VIc


We know the scene: the room, variously furnished,
almost always a lectern, a book; always
the tall lily.
            Arrived on solemn grandeur of great wings,
the angelic ambassador, standing or hovering,
whom she acknowledges, a guest.

But we are told of meek obedience. No one mentions
courage.
            The engendering Spirit
did not enter her without consent.
                            God waited.

She was free
to accept or to refuse, choice
integral to humanness.

———————————

Aren't there annunciations
of one sort or another
in most lives?
            Some unwillingly
undertake great destinies,
enact them in sullen pride,
uncomprehending.
        More often
those moments
    when roads of light and storm
    open from darkness in a man or woman,
are turned away from
in dread, in a wave of weakness, in despair
and with relief.
Ordinary lives continue.
                    God does not smite them.
But the gates close, the pathway vanishes.

———————————

She had been a child who played, ate, slept
like any other child – but unlike others,
wept only for pity, laughed
in joy not triumph.
Compassion and intelligence
fused in her, indivisible.

Called to a destiny more momentous
than any in all of Time,
she did not quail,
                    only asked
a simple, 'How can this be?'
and gravely, courteously,
took to heart the angel's reply,
perceiving instantly
the astounding ministry she was offered:

to bear in her womb
Infinite weight and lightness; to carry
in hidden, finite inwardness,
nine months of Eternity; to contain
in slender vase of being,
the sum of power –
in narrow flesh,
the sum of light.
                    Then bring to birth,
push out into air, a Man-child
needing, like any other,
milk and love –

but who was God.

This was the minute no one speaks of,
when she could still refuse.

A breath unbreathed,
                    Spirit,
                                suspended,
                                        waiting.

---

She did not cry, 'I cannot, I am not worthy,'
nor, 'I have not the strength.'
She did not submit with gritted teeth,
                              raging, coerced.
Bravest of all humans,
                    consent illumined her.
The room filled with its light,
the lily glowed in it,
                    and the iridescent wings.
Consent,
        courage unparalleled,
opened her utterly.

# Wings in the Pedlar's Pack

The certainty of wings: a child's bold heart,
not, good little *Schul*-boy, Torah or Talmud
gave it to you, a practical vision:
wings were needed, why should people
plod forever on foot, not glide like herons
through the blue and white
promise unfolding
over their heads, over
the river's thawing?
Therefore the pedlar. (But why did they not
avail themselves of his wares?)

My father, as a child, sees the magic pedlar Marc Chagall was also to see a few years later. The one intuited that he carried wings, the other painted him, wingless but floating high over Vitepsk.

Later, *ochetz moy*, when you discovered
wings for your soul, the same bold heart
empowered you. From Prussia east and southward
*verst* after *verst* you willed the train to go faster,
skimming the rails home to the Dnieper valley.
You bore such news, so longed-for,
fulfilling a hope so ancient
it had almost become dry parchment,
                          not hope any more.
At the station you hailed a *droshky*,
greeted the driver like a brother. At last
there was the street, there was the house:
but when you arrived
they would not listen.
They laughed at you. And then they wept.
But would not listen.

My father, as a student, discovers the Messiah,

and hurries home with the good news,

but is not believed.

# Inheritance

Even in her nineties she recalled
the smooth hands of the village woman
who sometimes came from down the street
and gently, with the softest
of soft old flannel,
soaped and rinsed and dried
her grubby face, while upstairs
the stepmother lay abed bitterly sleeping,
the uncorked opiate bottle
wafting out sticky sweetness
into a noontime dusk.
Those hands, that slow refreshment,
were so kind, I too,
another lifetime beyond them,
shall carry towards my death
their memory,
grateful, and longing
once again to feel them soothe me.

# Nativity: An Altarpiece

The wise men are still on the road, searching,
crowns and gifts packed in their saddlebags.

The shepherds are still asleep on the hill, their woolen
caps pulled over their ears, their campfire low.

It's the wondering animals, ox and ass, unused
to human company after dark, who witness,

alone with Mary and Joseph, the birth; who hear
the cry, the first cry

of earthly breath drawn through the newborn lungs
of God.
         And the cord is cut, and the shepherds
that selfsame moment have sprung to their feet

in a golden shower of angels, terrified, then
rejoicing. They lope downhill to the barn

to see their Redeemer. A cloud of
celestial music surrounds them.

                      The wise men
are still far off, alone on the road with a star.

But the ox and the ass
are kneeling already, the Family's oldest friends,

in the glow of light that illumines the byre, the straw,
their eyes and the human eyes – a glow

shed from no source but the living Child Himself.

## The Open Sentence

To look out over roofs
of a different city –

steaming tiles, chimney pots, mansards,
the gleam on distant spires
after a downpour –

To look out
(and the air freshens)
and say to oneself,
*Today…*

## The Past (I)

Somewhere, married and in love,
we walked through streets planted with linden trees.
There were ramparts, buttresses, ancient fragments
bonded with newer masonry that was old too.
The warmth of the day just ending
stretched itself on the stones, a golden dog.
People were strolling, there were no cars to speak of,
and we, we were only passing through.
What chance imperative held us on course
toward what train? Nothing I can remember,
no better city.
                Quiet avenues. Lamps coming on.
The sky still full of light.
I can't remember arriving nor leaving,
and even while we were there it seems
we were somewhere else, inattentive. But the lindens
were blossoming, their perfume, mysterious, pianissimo,
filled the whole town: every few years that remembrance
briefly returns, as if
a fragment of dream; but I know
it was history, a bit of my life,
a bit of the life of Europe. The past.
We failed to linger – as if the lindens
only spoke over this gulf of time.

# A Calvary Path

Where the stone steps
falter and come to an end
but the hillside rises
yet more steeply,
obtruded roots of the pines
have braided themselves
across the path to continue
the zigzag staircase.
In times past the non-human –
plants, animals –
often, with such gestures,
intervened in our lives,
or so our forebears
believed when all lives were seen
as travellings-forth of souls.
One can perceive
few come here now –
it's nothing special,
not even very old,
a naive piety,
artless, narrow. And yet
this ladder of roots
draws one onward, coaxing
feet to become
pilgrim feet, that climb
(silenced by layers
of fallen needles,
but step by step
held from sliding)
up to the last
cross of the calvary.

# The Past (II)

*The witnesses are old things, undimmed, dense*
*With the life of human hands*
CZESLAW MILOSZ

My hand on chiseled stone, fitting
into the invisible
                    print of the mason's own
                    where it lay
a moment of that year the nave
was still half-risen, roofless...

There's a past that won't suffice:
years in billions,
walls of strata. My need roams
history, centuries not aeons.
And replica is useless.

The new dust
floated past, his mate
from the scaffolding reached down
for the water-jug.

                    This stone
or another: no inch of all
untouched. Cold, yes,

but that human trace
will burn my palm.
This is a hunger.

# Reflections

The mountain trembles in the dark lake,
its golden cliffs dipping
from almost-sunset light
deep into almost-evening waters.
Round them the forest
floats, brushstrokes
                    blurred just a little.

Death and the past
move closer, move
away again and once more
come closer, swaying, unhurried,
like the sound
of cowbells wandering
down the steep pastures.

# Midnight Gladness

*Peace be upon each thing my eye takes in,*
*Upon each thing my mouth takes in.*
                CARMINA GADELICA

The pleated lampshade, slightly askew,
dust a silverish muting of the lamp's fake brass.
My sock-monkey on the pillow, tail and limbs asprawl,
weary after a day of watching sunlight
                prowl the house like a wolf.
Gleams of water in my bedside glass.
Miraculous water, so peacefully
waiting to be consumed.

The day's crowding arrived
at this abundant stillness. Each thing
given to the eye before sleep, and water
at my lips before darkness. Gift after gift.

VI

## St Thomas Didymus

In the hot street at noon I saw him
                      a small man
    gray but vivid, standing forth
                          beyond the crowd's buzzing
holding in desperate grip his shaking
                       teethgnashing son,

and thought him my brother.

I heard him cry out, weeping, and speak
                       those words,
Lord, I believe, help thou
            mine unbelief,

and knew him
       my twin:

a man whose entire being
             had knotted itself
into the one tightdrawn question,
                 Why,
why has this child lost his childhood in suffering,
       why is this child, who will soon be a man,
tormented, torn, twisted?
           Why is he cruelly punished
who has done nothing except be born?

The twin of my birth
          was not so close
as that man I heard
        say what my heart
sighed with each beat, my breath silently
               cried in and out,
in and out.

After the healing,
       he, with his wondering
newly peaceful boy, receded;
         no one

dwells on the gratitude, the astonished joy,
                              the swift
acceptance and forgetting.
                    I did not follow
to see their changed lives.
                    What I retained
was the flash of kinship.
                    Despite
all that I witnessed,
                    his question remained
my question, throbbed like a stealthy cancer,
                              known
only to doctor and patient. To others
                              I seemed well enough.

So it was
          that after Golgotha
                    my spirit in secret
lurched in the same convulsed writhings
                              that tore that child
before he was healed.
                    And after the empty tomb
when they told me He lived, had spoken to Magdalen,
                              told me
that though He had passed through the door like a ghost
                    He had breathed on them
the breath of a living man –
                    even then
when hope tried with a flutter of wings
                              to lift me –
still, alone with myself,
                    my heavy cry was the same: *Lord,*
*I believe,*
          *help thou mine unbelief.*

I needed
          blood to tell me the truth,
the touch
          of blood. Even
my sight of the dark crust of it
                    round the nailholes

didn't thrust its meaning all the way through
                                         to that manifold knot in me
that willed to possess all knowledge,
                                 refusing to loosen
unless that insistence won
                         the battle I fought with life.

But when my hand
                 led by His hand's firm clasp
entered the unhealed wound,
                                 my fingers encountering
rib-bone and pulsing heat,
                         what I felt was not
scalding pain, shame for my
                         obstinate need,
but light, light streaming
                         into me, over me, filling the room
as if I had lived till then
                         in a cold cave, and now
coming forth for the first time,
                         the knot that bound me unravelling,
I witnessed
         all things quicken to color, to form,
my question
         not answered but given
                         its part
in a vast unfolding design lit
                 by a risen sun.

# Dream Cello

When he improvised, from what
unpremeditated congeries of wisdoms
did the sounds appear, woven
like laser tracings on the screen of air?
Music out of 'nowhere,' that granary,
that palace of Arabian serpents,
of sleek rats plush as
young seals. What do words, too,
do there, the real ones,
while we dally with their pale
understudies, or swim
through choppy floods, too busy
with breathing to summon them?
Could we live there? Is it dark?
Could the grain shoals
not light us with their gold sheen?
Invisible hive, has it no small door
we could find if we stood
quite still and listened?

# Ikon: The Harrowing of Hell

Down through the tomb's inward arch
He has shouldered out into Limbo
to gather them, dazed, from dreamless slumber:
the merciful dead, the prophets,
the innocents just His own age and those
unnumbered others waiting here
unaware, in an endless void He is ending
now, stooping to tug at their hands,
to pull them from their sarcophagi,
dazzled, almost unwilling. Didmas,
neighbor in death, Golgotha dust
still streaked on the dried sweat of his body
no one had washed and anointed, is here,
for sequence is not known in Limbo;
the promise, given from cross to cross
at noon, arches beyond sunset and dawn.
All these He will swiftly lead
to the Paradise road: they are safe.
That done, there must take place that struggle
no human presumes to picture:
living, dying, descending to rescue the just
from shadow, were lesser travails
than this: to break
through earth and stone of the faithless world
back to the cold sepulchre, tearstained
stifling shroud; to break from *them*
back into breath and heartbeat, and walk
the world again, closed into days and weeks again,
wounds of His anguish open, and Spirit
streaming through every cell of flesh
so that if mortal sight could bear
to perceive it, it would be seen
His mortal flesh was lit from within, now,
and aching for home. He must return,
first, in Divine patience, and know
hunger again, and give
to humble friends the joy
of giving Him food – fish and a honeycomb.

*(Lent 1988)*

104

## Variation on a Theme by Rilke
*(The Book of Hours, Book I, #15)*


With chips and shards, rubble of being,
we construct
            not You but our hope of You.
We say – we dustmotes in the cosmos –
'You dome, arching above us!':
as if You were the sanctuary
by which we seek to define You.

Our cities pulverize, proud technologies
spawn catastrophe. The jaws of our inventions
snap down and lock.
                Their purpose will be forgotten;
Time is aeons
and we live in minutes,
flies on a windowpane.

Who can conceive the span of You,
great vault, ribbed cauldron slung beneath the abyss,
cage of eternity?

Metaphors shatter, mirrors of poverty.

But something in us, while the millennia
monotonously pass
                and pass,
hungers to offer up
our specks of life as fragile tesserae
towards the vast mosaic – temple, eidolon;

to be, ourselves, imbedded in its fabric,
as if, once, it was from that we were broken off.

# EVENING TRAIN

# 1 Lake Mountain Moon

## Settling

I was welcomed here – clear gold
of late summer, of opening autumn,
the dawn eagle sunning himself on the highest tree,
the mountain revealing herself unclouded, her snow
tinted apricot as she looked west,
tolerant, in her steadfastness, of the restless sun
forever rising and setting.
                              Now I am given
a taste of the grey foretold by all and sundry,
a grey both heavy and chill. I've boasted I would not care,
I'm London-born. And I won't. I'll dig in,
into my days, having come here to live, not to visit.
Grey is the price
of neighboring with eagles, of knowing
a mountain's vast presence, seen or unseen.

# Elusive

The mountain comes and goes
on the horizon,

        a rhythm elusive as that of a sea-wave
        higher than all the rest, riding to shore
        flying its silver banners –

you count to seven, but no,
its measure
        slips by you with each recurrence.

# Morning Mist

The mountain absent,
a remote folk-memory.

The peninsula
vanished, hill, trees –
gone, shoreline
a rumour.

And we equate
God with these absences –
Deus absconditus.
But God

is imaged
as well or better
in the white stillness

resting everywhere,

giving to all things
an hour of Sabbath,

no leaf stirring,
the hidden places

tranquil in solitude.

## Presence

Though the mountain's the same warm-tinted ivory
as the clouds (as if a red ground had been laid beneath
not quite translucent white) and though the clouds
disguise its shoulders, and rise tall to left and right,
and soften the pale summit with mist,
                                    yet one perceives
the massive presence, obdurate, unconcerned
among those filmy guardians.

# Effacement

Today the mountain
is cloud,
pale cone of shadow
veiled by a paler scrim –

majestic presence become
one cloud among others,
humble vapor,
barely discernible,

like the archangel walking
with Tobias on dusty roads.

# Heron (I)

St Simon Heron,
standing, standing, standing
upon his offshore pillar,

suddenly, subtly
dips his head to drink,
three, then a fourth,
and more times, that legato
arabesque of the neck,
the small head almost a serpent's,
smoothly one with its flexible stem.
Body and tall legs
move not an inch.
                          Hunger,
thirst, fulfillment
are ripples that lap his surface;
his patience absorbs them.
Time does not pass, for him;
it is the lake, and full, and still,
and he has all of it, and wades to strike
when he will upon his fish.

# Heron (II)

Elegantly gray, the blue heron
rises from perfect stillness on wide wings,
            flies a few beats
      sideways,
                  trails his feet in the lake,
      and rises again to circle
from marker to marker (the posts
that show where the bottom shelves downward)
choosing:
and lands on the floating dock where the gulls cluster –

a tall prince come down from the castle to walk,
proud and awkward, in the market square,
while squat villagers
break off their deals
and look askance.

# Taking Charge

Here comes the moon,
bright rim
slicing importantly
through windrows of
grey thistledown cloud just losing
their sundown flush.

## Abruptly

The last warm day, I caught,
almost unnoticing,
        that high shrilling like thin
wires of spun silver, glint
of wheeling flight – some small tribe
leaving.
                        That night
the moon was full; by morning
autumn had come.

# October Moonrise

### 1

Moon, wisp of opal fire, then slowly
revealed as orb arising,
still half-hidden; the dark
bulk of the wooded ridge defined
by serrations of pine and fir against
this glow
       that begins to change
from lambent red to a golden
pervasive mist of light as the whole
fullness of moon
floats clear of the hill.

### 2

Risen, the gold moon
will shrink and blanch
but for now, still
low in the sky,

her pallor is veiled
as if by a net of
gilded gossamer

and the path she has laid down
over the ripples of
dark lake water

is gold unalloyed.

## Daily Bread

A gull far-off
rises and falls, arc of a breath,
two sparrows pause on the telephone wire,
chirp a brief interchange, fly back to the ground,
the bus picks up one passenger and zooms on up the hill,
across the water the four poplars
conceal their tremor, feet together, arms pressed to their sides,
behind them the banked conifers dark and steep;
my peartree drops a brown pear from its inaccessible height
into the bramble and ivy tangle, grey sky
whitens a little, now one can see vague forms of cloud
pencilled lightly across it.
*This is the day that the Lord hath made,*
*let us rejoice and be glad in it.*

## Open Secret

Perhaps one day I shall let myself
approach the mountain –
hear the streams which must flow down it,
lie in a flowering meadow, even
touch my hand to the snow.
Perhaps not. I have no longing to do so.
I have visited other mountain heights.
This one is not, I think, to be known
by close scrutiny, by touch of foot or hand
or entire outstretched body; not by any
familiarity of behavior, any acquaintance
with its geology or the scarring roads
humans have carved in its flanks.
This mountain's power
lies in the open secret of its remote
apparition, silvery low-relief
coming and going moonlike at the horizon,
always loftier, lonelier, than I ever remember.

# II  The Two Magnets

# The Two Magnets

Where broken gods, faded saints, (powerful in antique presence
as old dancers with straight backs, loftily confident,
or old men in threadbare wellcut coats) preside casually
over the venerable conversations of cypress and olive,
there intrudes, like a child interrupting, tugging at my mind,
incongruous, persistent,
the image of young salmon in round ponds at the hatchery
across an ocean and a continent, circling
with muscular swiftness – tints of green, pink, blue,
glowing mysteriously through slate gray, under trees
unknown here, whose names I forget because
they were unknown to me too when I was young.

And there on the western edge of America – home to me now,
and calling me with this image of something I love,
yet still unknown – I dream of cathedrals,
of the worn stone of human centuries.
Guarded by lions with blunted muzzles
or griffins verdant with moss, gateposts open in me
to effaced avenues.
Part of me lives under nettle-grown foundations.
Part of me wanders west and west, and has reached
the edge of the mist where salmon wait the day
when something shall lift them and give them to deeper waters.

## Steadfast

Tattooed in black and gold, lichened nymphs,
sentinels faithful to their garden wall,
face the impertinent back of a new villa,
their view of the lake usurped.

# Stele
*(I-II c. B.C.)*


They part at the edge of substance.
Henceforth, he will be shadow
in a land of shadow.
And she – she too will be going
slowly down a road of cloud,
weightless, untouched, untouching.
This is the last crossroad.
Her right hand and his left
are clasped, but already,
muffled in his acceptance of fate,
his attention recedes from her.
Her left hand rises, fingertips trace
the curve of his warm face
as it cools and fades.
He has looked down his road,
he is ready to go, not willingly
yet without useless resistance.
She too accepts the truth, there is no way back,
but she has not looked, yet, at the path
accorded to her. She has not given herself,
not yet, to her shadowhood.

# The Faithful Lover

Play with a few decades, shift them:
try to imagine Ruskin in the New World,
walking with John Muir in the wilderness.

He, whose enraptured first sight of the Alps
transformed him, that meek Protestant Sunday
when he and Mama and Papa and dull cousin Mary
were patiently waiting the secular week's beginning
before attempting the sights,
                            but all unawares
came face to face
with the sublime – unmistakeably not clouds,
surpassing all that engravings had promised,
floating west of Schaffhausen, sharp, *tinged with rose –*
*far into blue – suddenly – beyond!*

– changed him from docile prig (poor child: he was 14 and knew
so much and so little) to a man of passion,
whatever his failings.

Imagine him in Yosemite. Would loyalties already divided
– Rock Simple or Rock Wrought,
strata of mountains, strata of human craft,
tools of Geology or tools of Art – have split him?
Would wilderness, legends unknown, or if known offering
no toe-hold for his mind's expectant footing,
have swept him wholly into its torrents of non-human grandeur?

Or wouldn't Art have pulled him back in the end
to layered history felt in the bones,
(even Geology a fraction of that insistence, loved
for its poetry of form, color, textures,
not as a scientist loves it)?
Back to where human hands created
*rich tessellations* or the *shadowy Rialto*
*threw its colossal curve slowly*
*forth...that strange curve, so delicate,*
*so adamantine, strong as a mountain cavern,*
*graceful as a bow just bent – ?*

Back to where Nature – even the Alps, still so remote,
unsung through so many centuries –

lay in the net or nest of perception,
seen then re-seen, recognized, wrought in myth.

# A Little Visit to Doves and Chickens
*(for Page Smith)*


Demure and peaceful, quiet above
the crooning chickens (who peck and strut,
equally peaceful in winter sun, a level below them,
as if on the ground-floor of a two-storey house),
the doves
are softly pale: gray warmed by brown;
and each one wears a collar, narrow and black
as the velvet ribbon girls and dowagers
used to clasp at the throat with a diamond.
Unlike their cousins the city pigeons,
they don't seem obsessed by sex or food,
don't chase one another in circles,
don't keep talking. They are as calm
in motion as in repose.
                        The chickens meanwhile
remind me of wealthy peasants
in an ancient culture – their rustic finery, gold,
scarlet, opulent umber, brighter and just as beautiful
as the doves' patrician sobriety, and their manners
good but less formal. Their comforts
are earned by their labors. One wonders
if from the doves also their keeper extracts a tithe,
or retains them merely to be
their dreamy selves.

No, there's no moral nor irony
lurking among these words, no message –
unless the sense
                that it's pleasant to visit a while
                a modest, indeed a minute, poultry yard
                where such content may be witnessed
                and even a pair of guineafowl don't seem nervous
is itself a message simply because
it's wistful, the leisure of mind
to lean on the fence and simply look, and not feel
the need to press for a subtext, being so rare.

# The Composition
*(for Jean Joubert and for Howard Fussiner)*

*Woman at the Harpsichord, Emmanuel de Witte, 1617-1692, Musée des Beaux Arts, Montreal*

Two rooms away, seen through the open door,
the servant-maid raises her head to listen,
times the strokes of her broom to the music's crisp
golden wavelets. Autumn sun
and shadows well-defined overlay the floortiles,
antiphonal transverse strips over squares
of white and black. Filtered through little panes
in long and lofty windows, the light
hints at green in its morning pallor. But red,
red is the lord of color here: the draperies,
bedside carpet, ceiling-beams, elaborate
hanging lamp, a chair, all these and more
are a glowing Indian red; and red above all,
with its canopy, valance, ample curtains,
the big four-poster. Up and dressed, the young wife,
(white cap and dimly auburn skirts, red jacket
basqued with ermine-tips) is playing
the harpsichord, beginning the day with delight,
while snug, still, in the bed's half-dark reclines
the young husband, leaning his head on one hand,
intently, blissfully, watching and listening.
A human scene: apex of civilized joy, attained
in Holland, the autumn of 1660, never surpassed, probably
never to be matched.
                              But if
the same scene had been painted differently –
not only with other colors but from another
distance, perspectives differently disposed, more curves,
less play of severe rectangles; if it had been
a composition that lacked this austere
counterpoint of forms which evoke,
in brave resplendent red, the very
twang and trill and wiry
ground bass of the notes ringing forth
under her fingers – if it had been
reduced to anecdote – we'd never have known
that once, in eternity,
this peaceful joy had blessed an autumnal morning.

130

# III Ancient Airs

## Broken Pact

A face ages quicker than a mind.

And thighs, arms, breasts,
take on an air of indifference.
Heart's desire has wearied them, they choose to forget
whatever they once promised.

But mind and heart continue
their eager conversation,
they argue, they share epiphanies,
sometimes all night they raise
antiphonal laments.

Face and body have betrayed them,

they are alone together,
unsure how to proceed.

# Diptych

## 1. *Mysterious Movement*

Though no wind is blowing, the lake,
       as if to reënact the remote day
       when, as a journeying river, it first flowed
       into the long hollow of its bed
       and met the embracing shores
       and could go no further,
is pressing strongly, darkly,
southward in fading light, this waning hour
near the close of the year –

although it can go no further.

## 2. *Midwinter*

A sky stained
even at midmorning
with the water and blood of daybreak...

And the mountain,
strangely approachable
this winter day,
has moved forward into the middle distance,
humbly letting valleys and dark
seams of rock be perceived,
like a woman not trying to hide
her loss of youth from the light.
Her snows are gray.

# Ancient Airs and Dances

1

I knew too well
what had befallen me
when, one night, I put my lips to his wineglass
after he left – an impulse I thought was locked away with a smile
into memory's museum.

When he took me to visit friends and the sea, he lay
asleep in the next room's dark where the fire
rustled all night; and I, from a warm bed, sleepless,
watched through the open door
that glowing hearth, and heard,
drumming the roof, the rain's
insistent heartbeat.

Greyhaired, I have not grown wiser,
unless to perceive absurdity
is wisdom. A powerless wisdom.

II

Shameless heart! Did you not vow to learn
        stillness from the heron,
        quiet from the mists of fall,
        and from the mountain – what was it?
        Pride? Remoteness?
You have forgotten already!
And now you clamor again
like an obstinate child demanding attention,
interrupting study and contemplation.
You try my patience. Bound as we are
together for life, must you now,
so late in the day, go bounding sideways,
trying to drag me with you?

# Time for Rivets

Reinforced though it was
with stoic strapping,
my heart was breaking again. Damn!
Just when I had so much to do,
a list as long as your arm.
The world news slithered
toward the probable worst
of a lifetime's bad news,
and as for me (as if in that shadow it mattered —
but it did) in two day's time
I'd be saying goodbye to someone I thought of
'day and night,' as I'd not been planning to think
of anyone ever again.

I'd believed it would hold, yes,
I'd considered my serviceable heart
long-since well-mended,
and equal to what demands
might still confront it.
And hadn't I written, still longer ago,
that these metaphorical hearts, although
they 'break for nothing,' do so
in surface fissures only, a web
of hairline fractures, the way
old pieplates do, rimmed with a blue design
as if someone had pressed them all round
with tines of a fork well-dipped in indigo?
All true enough, but surely by now
mine, though made like such plates
for use, not show, must need
those clamps of metal with which
cracked vessels of finer porcelain are held.
For the moment I'd have to make do
with tape and crossed fingers.

# Arrived

Away from home,
the reality of home
evades me. Chairs,
sofa, table, a cup –
I can enumerate objects
one by one, but they're inventory,
not Gestalt. This house
I've stayed in often before,
the open suitcase,
my friends who live here,
that's what's real.
And that face
so vivid to me these past three months
evades me too: the shape
of his head, or
color of his eyes appear
at moments, but I can't
assemble feature with feature.
I seem to have landed
upon this *now*
as if on a mid-ocean island,
past and future two continents, both
lost in immense distance,
the mist and seasons
of months at sea – the voyage
from yesterday to today.

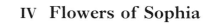

IV  Flowers of Sophia

# Range

Peak upon peak, brown, dustily gold, crowded,
sharp juttings, razorbacks, angular undulations,
so many we seem not to move above them, confusion
of multitudinous upthrust forms, pushing
against one another, surging.
                                    Valley forests
look from the air like dark green water,
but if there are lakes
they are hidden. A dry country
unless when the snows melt.

But at last
when a true lake shows itself
it is blue, blue, blue,
a cupful of sky.

## The Plains

Tiepolo clouds –
tinge of beige in diaphanous shadow
over cornfields and western bluffs
where no one has seen
how they hang also above
ascensions, veils,
ecstatic saints and the heads
of cherubim...

## Down Under

Bloodred, viridian, poison aqua:
round mineral pools or pits in the Nullarbor.
My photo, taken through scratched glass from the air,
was to have been a gift for an artist son,
but came out blurred and pale
and was never given.
                    Years later,
flying above a different desert,
I see with mind's eye the painting I imagined
he might have made from the pattern's
aboriginal mystery.

# Milky Way

Sky-wave breaks
in surf, and leaves
the lace of it to border
an obscure, ethereal,
sinuous coastline –

phosphorescent for that lingering
instant which is to us
time immemorial.

# Eye Mask

In this dark I rest,
unready for the light which dawns
day after day,
eager to be shared.
Black silk, shelter me.
I need
more of the night before I open
eyes and heart
to illumination. I must still
grow in the dark like a root
not ready, not ready at all.

# Entre Loup et Chien

Night's broken wing
and its wide untorn one
hobble across the paling sky
dropping black feathers down on black trees.
Day is still forming itself.
This is the gap,
the time between the sagacious, taciturn wolf
and the plain dog who will yap into place
when dawn has flared and faded.

## On the Eve
*(for Melanie)*

The moon was white
in the stillness. Daylight
changed without moving,
a hint of sundown
stained the sky. We walked
the short grass,
the dry ground of the hill,
beholding
the tinted west. We talked
of change in our lives. The moon
tuned its whiteness a tone higher.

# River

Dreaming the sea that
                    lies beyond me
I have enough depth
                    to know I am shallow.

I have my pools, my bowls
                    of rock I flow
into and fill, but I must
                    brim my own banks, persist,
vanish at last in greater flood
                    yet still within it
follow my task,
                    dreaming towards
the calling sea.

# Brother Ivy

Between road and sidewalk, the broadleafed ivy,
unloved, dusty, littered, sanctuary of rats,
gets on with its life. New leaves shine gaily
among dogged older ones
that have lost their polish.
It does not require appreciation. The foliage
conceals a brown tangle of stems
thick as a mangrove swamp; the roots
are spread tenaciously. Unwatered
throughout the long droughts, it simply
grips the dry ground by the scruff of the neck.

I am not its steward.
If we are siblings, and I
my brother's keeper therefore,
the relation is reciprocal. The ivy
meets its obligation by pure
undoubtable being.

# Idyll

The neighbor's Black Labrador, his owners
out at work, unconscious anyone
is watching him, rises again and again
on hind legs to bend with his paws
the figtree's curving branches
and reach the sweet figs with his black lips.

## Arctic Spring

The polar she-bear, dirty ivory
against the blue-white steep
slope of ice
rolls and slides like a cub,
happy to stretch cramped limbs after four
months in the stuffy den;
but quickly lopes
upward with toed-in undulant grace
back to the bleating summons
of three new bears, their first time out,
hind feet still in the tunnel,
black astonished eyes regarding
their mother at play, black noses
twitching, smelling
strange wonders of air and light.

# Flowers of Sophia

Flax, chicory, scabious –
flowers with ugly names,
they grow in waste ground, sidewalk edges,
fumes, grime, trash.
Each kind has a delicate form, distinctive;
it would be pleasant to draw them.
All are a dreamy blue,
a gentle mysterious blue,
wise beyond comprehension.

# V  Evening Train

# In Love

Over gin and tonic (an unusual treat) the ancient poet
haltingly – not because mind and memory
        falter, but because language, now,
        weary from so many years
        of intense partnership,
        comes stiffly to her summons,
        with unsure footing –
recounts, for the first time in my hearing, each step
of that graceful sarabande, her husband's
last days, last minutes, fifteen years ago.

She files her belongings freestyle, jumbled
in plastic bags – poems, old letters, ribbons,
old socks, an empty pictureframe;
but keeps her fifty years of marriage wrapped, flawless,
in something we sense and almost see –
diaphanous as those saris one can pass through a wedding ring.

## Venerable Optimist

He saw the dark as a ragged garment
spread out to air.
Through its rents and moth-holes
the silver light came pouring.

# Letter to a Friend

As if we were sitting as we have done so often,
over a cup of tea, and I knew how
to read the leaves, let me look closely into
this card you have sent, this image you say
holds for you something you feel is yourself.
A woman sits outdoors by a white-cloth'd table
(blue in shadow); but it's not a café;
there are columns, masonry, perhaps a ruin behind her,
and also a stretch of open lawn or pasture,
and trees beyond. She has opened – a parasol?
or an umbrella? There's enough light to suggest
a parasol, but the coat she wears
is not for summer: passionate red is muted
almost to russet, and high collar, sleeves
that narrow from elbow to wrist, imply weight,
warm cloth. Yet the silken shelter's pale cerulean,
shot with gold, seems too light for rain.
Perhaps it is rainbow weather, flying showers
on a gleaming day in spring.
Not a young girl any more, this woman's
fresh color and shining hair are not yet
beginning to fade; but in her eyes one sees
knowledge, though in their clear, steady,
almost challenging gaze there's a certain innocence;
and her lips are firmly closed. Bareheaded,
(despite her coat) she is quietly seated,
not poised to leave; one arm rests on the chair's
green embracing arm.
                    Most notable in this portrait:
her solitude. She may or may not be waiting for someone;
whether or not, she looks out from the picture-plane
not at the painter but straight through time
at me looking back at her. She's not sad,
not angry, not joyful: but open, open
to what shall befall.
                    The image is only
a detail, fragment of a larger whole.
The context might change my reading. Companions
perhaps are nearby, unseen by us; perhaps she too

doesn't see them. The place she is in
might be defined if one saw the rest of the painting.
One might deduce from it why she is there,
where she will go. But the more I look, the more
I perceive what her eyes express: it's courage.
That's what told me this woman is innocent but not ignorant.
Courage knows the price of living. Courage itself
is a form of innocence, of trust or faith.
Your sense of being portrayed no doubt refers
to less than this; to her solitude, it may be.
It's against the rules to tell your own fortune,
and I, after all, am able only to descry
the images in the leaves, not to construe their meaning.
Some day one of us may discover the painting's whereabouts,
see the whole of it. Then we'll divine
what fortune her gaze betokens.

# Becca

Becca. Each washday,
steamy scullery, yellow soap-smell, whites
boiled in the copper. Becca brandishing
a stick, huge spoon to stir the bubbling
soup of linens.
A child had best keep out of the way.
And skreak of the mangle turning
hurt to hear.
Outdoors, though,
clotheslines made streets across the lawn,
walled with sheets, a billowing village.
Becca, bandy-legged, sturdy
under the weight, brought forth
the round wicker basket,
stretched wet
huge arms to the line to peg,
with gypsy pegs that stuffed
her apron pockets, more and more
clean clothes, mangle-wrung,
and the washday wind
slapped them, slapped
me as I dodged from door to invisible door, Becca
shouting, but not at me,
she was deaf I think, I think we never
exchanged a word, she just
appeared and then it was washday, but not
after I was six, perhaps five, perhaps four, yes,
early – for me she existed
at our washtub only, and in our garden,
with no in-between, no home, no story,
toothlessly smiling (not at me).
Lodged in my head
forever, primordial. Becca.
Known. Unknown.

# For Bet

You danced ahead of me, I took
none of those last steps with you
when your *enchainement* led you
uphill to the hospital and a death sentence
or before that when language
twirled round and tripped your voice.
Dancers must learn to walk
slowly across a stage, unfaltering;
we practiced that, long ago.
You faltered, but only in the wings,
that week when *timor mortis*
lunged at you. And you shook off
that devouring terror, held up
your head, straightened
your back, and moved in grace
(they tell me – I was not at your side
but far away,
intent on a different music)
into the light of that last stage,
a hospice garden, where you could say,
breathing the ripened fragrance of August mornings,
'yes, and evenings too are beautiful.'

# Link

Half memory of what my mother
at over ninety could still see
clear in mind's eye, transferring,
like earrings or brooches,
her lapidary trove
into my vision; half imprint
of that charcoal-burner with his boy,
gazing at thickets towering up
around the sleeping palace
in my childhood treasure of treasures,
Dulac's Perrault,
             I carry
into this alien epoch, year by year,
the presence of that venerable great-
or great-great uncle to whom,
precociously observant five-year-old,
she was taken one summer day
and told to remember always
that *he* could remember Waterloo,
when he was a drummer-boy, a lad
of twelve perhaps, and how Napoleon –
Boney, the bogeyman disobedient children
were threatened with – rode off on his mountainous
black horse.

The ancient's dark nets were spread
before his cottage; drowsing waves
lapped the Welsh strand and his beached coracle,
reflections wavering on the brilliant whitewash.
White hair grew to his shoulders, kneebritches left
his brown legs bare, his feet were bare.
Indoors, the earth floor, hard as flagstones,
had for ornament patterns he drew
with the staining juice of a certain plant.

             I perceive, seeing him there,
his life, glimpsed that day and held
in the amber pendant I inherit, belongs
to any of several centuries, though now

it has no place except in me, as if memory travelled
fingertip to outstretched fingertip
across the longest lives, an electric gesture
learned of Adam, dwindling
to meanings we no longer know,
but only know our sense of history
has only such barely-touchings, uninterpreted
not-forgettings, to suffice
for its continuance.

# The Opportunity

My father once, after his death,
appeared to me as a rose,
passed beyond intellect.
This time, he resumes
human form to become
a boy of six.
I kneel to hug him,
kiss the child's bare shoulder;
near us the ocean
sighs and murmurs,
firm sand reflects
the turn of the wave.

This is my chance to tell him,
'Much has happened, over the years,
many travels.
In the world,
in myself.
Along the way,
I have come to believe
the truth of what you believe.'

The child, with good grace,
permits
my brief embrace; he smiles:
the words
are lazy waves above and around him,
he absorbs their tone,
knows he is loved.
Knows only that.

This was my chance
to speak, I've taken it,
we are both content.

# Dream Instruction

In the language-root place (a wooden
hall, homestead; warm, Homeric, Beowulfian shelter)
candles are glowing, shadows in rhythm
rise and fall. Into this haven have swept,
blown by gusting winds, figures whose drama
makes a stage, for a while, of place and time,
enthralling attention, prompting action,
so that my mind meshes itself in their story
until with promises, tears, laughter, they sweep
out once more into night. Ruefully,
'Life!' I stammer, as the wake of their passage
ebbs and vanishes, 'It rushes and rushes toward me
like Niagara – I don't have time
to write it, to write it down, to hold it, it never
pauses!'            And she whom I address,
the old mother sitting in bed, cheerful, spritely,
cushions behind her, saucer in one hand,
porcelain cup in the other, sipping her fragrant tea,
smiles in wisdom and tells me
that need will pass; she herself
has come to live in what happens, not in the telling.
She quotes to me what a woman
born in slavery said, when she was free and ancient:
*I sits here, in my rocker, evenin's,*
*and just*

      *purely*

         *be's.*

The vision
of mighty falls bearing down on me still
thundering in my mind, I see
a crimson candle guttering, flaring, and another, too,
whose wax is an amber yellow almost
the gold of its flame. Colors
of passionate life. I recall
*Out, out, brief candle.* 'Shall I snuff them?' 'Leave them –
they'll still themselves
as the air hushes.'

         I think of the travellers
gone into dark. 'They were only

passing through,' I say, surprised,
to her, to myself,
relieved and in awe, learning to know
those oncoming waters rushed through the aeons
before me, and rush on beyond me,
and I have now, as the task before me, to *be*,
to arrive at being,
as she the Old Mother has done
in the root place, the hewn
wooden cave, home
of shadow and flame, of
language, gradual stillness,
blessing.

# Evening Train

An old man sleeping in the evening train,
face upturned, mouth discreetly closed,
hands clasped, with fingers interlaced.
Those large hands
lie on the fur lining of his wife's coat
he's holding for her, and the fur
looks like a limp dog, docile and affectionate.
The man himself is a peasant
in city clothes, moderately prosperous –
rich by the standards of his youth;
one can read that in his hands,
his sleeping features.
How tired he is, how tired.
I called him old, but then I remember
my own age, and acknowledge he's likely
no older than I. But in the dimension
that moves with us but itself keeps still
like the bubble in a carpenter's level,
I'm fourteen, watching the faces I saw each day
on the train going in to London,
and never spoke to; or guessing
from a row of shoes what sort of faces
I'd see if I raised my eyes.
Everyone has an unchanging age (or sometimes two)
carried within them, beyond expression.
This man perhaps
is ten, putting in a few hours most days
in a crowded schoolroom, and a lot more
at work in the fields; a boy who's always
making plans to go fishing his first free day.
The train moves through the dark quite swiftly
(the Italian dark, as it happens)
with its load of people, each
with a conscious destination, each
with a known age and that other,

the hidden one – except for those
still young, or not young but slower to focus,
who haven't reached yet that state of being
which will become
not a point of arrest but a core
around which the mind develops, reflections circle,
events accrue – a center.
                              A girl with braids
sits in this corner seat, invisible,
pleased with her solitude. And across from her
an invisible boy, dreaming. She knows
she cannot imagine his dreams. Quite swiftly
we move through our lives; swiftly, steadily the train
rocks and bounces onward through sleeping fields,
our unknown stillness
holding level as water sealed in glass.

# VI Witnessing from Afar

# The Reminder

Composed by nature, time, human art,
an earthly paradise. A haze that is not smog
gentles the light. Mountains delicately frosted,
timbered autumnal hillsides copper and bronze.
Black-green of pine, gray-green of olive.
Nothing is missing. Ferries' long wakes pattern the water,
send to still shores a minor music of waves.
Dark perpendiculars
of cypress, grouped or single, cross immemorial
horizontals of terraced slopes, the outstretched wings,
creamy yellow, of villas more elegant
in slight disrepair than anything spick and span
ever could be. And all perceived
not through our own crude gaze alone but by the accretion
of others' vision – language, paint, memory transmitted.
Here, just now, the malady
we know the earth endures seems in remission –
or *we* are, from that knowledge that gnaws at us.
But only seems. Down by the lake the sign:
'Swim at your own risk. The lake is polluted.'
*Not badly,* someone says, blithely irrelevant.
We can avoid looking that way,
if we choose. That's at our own risk.
Deep underneath remission's fragile peace,
the misshaped cells remain.


*Lago di Como, 1989*

# Mysterious Disappearance of May's Past Perfect

Even as the beaches blacken again with oil,
reporters tell us, 'If the ship had had
a double hull, the spill
*may* not have occurred.' And now a poet
writing of one who died some years ago
too young, recounts that had she been and done
otherwise than she was and did, it's thought she
'*may* have survived.' The poet does not agree –
but this impoverished grammar, nonetheless,
places in doubt an undeniable death.
           Is it collective fear suppresses
*might* have, fear that causes do
produce effects? Does *may* still trail with it,
misused, a comforting openness, illusion
that what has already happened, after all
can be revoked, reversed?
                        Or, in these years
when from our mother-tongue some words
were carelessly tossed away, while others hastily
were being invented – chief among them, *overkill* –
has the other meaning, swollen as never before,
of *might* thrust out of memory its minor
homonym, so apt for the precise
nuance of elegy, for the hint of judgement,
reproachful clarities of tense and sense?

# Tragic Error

*The earth is the Lord's,* we gabbled,
*and the fullness thereof* –
while we looted and pillaged, claiming indemnity:
*the fullness thereof*
*given over to us, to our use* –
while we preened ourselves, sure of our power,
wilful or ignorant, through the centuries.

Miswritten, misread, that charge:
*subdue* was the false, the misplaced word in the story.
Surely we were to have been
earth's mind, mirror, reflective source.
Surely our task
was to have been
to love the earth,
to *dress and keep it* like Eden's garden.

*That* would have been our *dominion*:
to be those cells of earth's body that could
perceive and imagine, could bring the planet
into the haven it is to be known,
(as the eye blesses the hand, perceiving
its form and the work it can do).

# Mid-American Tragedy

They want to be their own old vision
of Mom and Dad. They want their dying son
to be eight years old again, not a gay man,
not ill, not dying. They have accepted him,
they would say if asked, unlike some who shut
errant sons out of house and heart,
and this makes them preen a little, secretly;
*but enough of that*, some voice within them
whispers, even more secretly, *he's our kid*,
*Mom and Dad are going to give him*
*what all kids long for, a trip to Disney World,*
*what fun, the best Xmas ever.*
And he, his wheelchair strung with bottles and tubes,
glass and metal glittering in winter sun,
shivers and sweats and tries to breathe as *Jingle Bells*
pervades the air and his mother, his father,
chatter and still won't talk, won't listen,
will never listen, never give him
the healing silence
in which they could have heard
his questions, his answers,
his life at last.

# The Batterers

A man sits by the bed
of a woman he has beaten,
dresses her wounds,
gingerly dabs at bruises.
Her blood pools about her,
darkens.

Astonished, he finds he's begun
to cherish her. He is terrified.
Why had he never
seen, before, what she was?
What if she stops breathing?

Earth, can we not love you
unless we believe the end is near?
Believe in your life
unless we think you are dying?

# Airshow Practice

Sinister wreathing mist in midsummer sky
slowly disperses
as it descends
over the wooded hill, the lake, the bathing children:

streaks of exhaust left by Blue Angels as they
scream back and forth, virtuosos of costly power,
swifter than hurricane –

to whom a multitude
gazes upward, craving
a violent awe, numb to all else.

# Watching TV

So many men – and not the worst of them,
the brutally corrupt, no, others,

liberal, intelligent if not
notably imaginative,

men with likeable eyes –

have mouths that are weak, cruel, twisted,
alien to desire:

mouths that don't match their eyes.

And our wretched history
utters through those mouths

the perfidies their hurt eyes evade.

## Protesters

Living on the rim
of the raging cauldron, disasters

witnessed but
not suffered in the flesh.

The choice: to speak
or not to speak.
We spoke.

Those of whom we spoke
had not that choice.

At every epicenter, beneath
roar and tumult,

enforced:
their silence.

# Hoping

All my life hoping the nightmare
I dreamed as a child (and could make recur
if perverse fascination willed it)
was not prophetic:
                    all the animals
seated in peaceful council by candleglow
in a shadowy, fragrant barn,
timeless, unmenaced – then without warning,
without any flash or noise,
the crumbling to black ash, ash
corrugated, writhing, as filmy shreds
of paper used to when sheets of it,
placed round the firescreen to coax the draft
upward and liven the coals, would themselves
catch fire and float, newsprint curdling,
dreadfully out from the hearth towards me.
All my life hoping; having to hope
because decades brought no reassurance.

# The Certainty

They have refined the means of destruction,
abstract science almost visibly shining,
it is so highly polished. Immaterial weapons
no one could ever hold in their hands
streak across darkness, across great distances,
threading through mazes to arrive
at targets that are concepts –

But one ancient certainty
remains: war
means blood spilling from living bodies,
means severed limbs, blindness, terror,
means grief, agony, orphans, starvation,
prolonged misery, prolonged resentment and hatred and guilt,
means all of these multiplied, multiplied,
means death, death, death and death.

# The Youth Program

The children have been practicing,
    diligent before their screens, playing
        a million missions a week.
A few teddybears, cuddly tigers, unicorns,
    still lie prone
        on youthbed pillows.
In antique-shops
    you may find sometimes
        a few small bows and arrows,
    Arthurian picturebooks,
        even cardboard theaters with cut-out
fairytale characters –
    Aladdin, Rose Red, Rose White –
        saved by chance from the garbage;
but the children
    don't even know such things
        gave pleasure once, and are gone.
They're busy with the new
    play-learning: they may not know
        the words *millenium, apocalypse,*
but the expensive games are already
    putting them ahead:
        pilots today, a spokesman says,
have attained
    new speeds of reflex,
        though trained on earlier models.
These children
    are preparing,
        being prepared.
But before their war
    begins,
        others, in which
their brothers, their young fathers
    will be deployed,
may have *taken out*
    the world.
        Perhaps someone
should tell the children, interrupt
    their wasted time?

Persuade them to run
outdoors for a while, and take
a look at the unfamiliar
while it is there —
*sky, tree, bird?* Or even
risk their annoyance and
turn off the power?

# Misnomer

They speak of the art of war,
but the arts
draw their light from the soul's well,
and warfare
dries up the soul and draws its power
from a dark and burning wasteland.
When Leonardo
set his genius to devising
machines of destruction he was not
acting in the service of art,
he was suspending
the life of art
over an abyss,
as if one were to hold
a living child out of an airplane window
at thirty thousand feet.

## Witnessing from Afar the New Escalation of Savage Power

She was getting old, had seen a lot,
knew a lot.
But something innocent
enlivened her,
upheld her spirits.
She tended a small altar,
kept a candle shielded there,
or tried to. There was a crash and throb
of harsh sound audible
always, but distant.
She believed
she had it in her
to fend for herself and hold
despair at bay.
Now when she came to the ridge and saw
the world's raw gash
reopened, the whole world
a valley of steaming blood,
her small wisdom
guttered in the uprush;
*rubbledust, meatpulse* –
darkness and the blast
levelled her. (Not her own death,
that was not yet.) The deafening
downrush. Shock, shame
no memory, no knowledge
nor dark imagination
had prepared her for.

*January–March 1991*

# News Report, September 1991

U.S. BURIED IRAQI SOLDIERS ALIVE IN GULF WAR

*'What you saw was a*
*bunch of trenches with*
*arms sticking out.'*
'Plows mounted on
tanks. Combat
earthmovers.'
'Defiant.'
'Buried.'
'Carefully planned and
rehearsed.'
*'When we*
*went through there wasn't*
*anybody left.'*
'Awarded
Silver Star.'
'Reporters
banned.'
'Not a single
American killed.'
'Bodycount
impossible.'
*'For all I know,*
*thousands,* said
Colonel Moreno.'
*'What you*
*saw was a bunch of*
*buried trenches*
*with people's*
*arms and things*
*sticking out.'*
'Secretary Cheney
made no mention.'
'Every single American
was inside
the juggernaut
impervious
to small-arms

180

fire.' *'I know*
*burying people*
*like that sounds*
*pretty nasty*, said
Colonel Maggart,
*But...* '
'His force buried
about six hundred
and fifty
in a thinner line
of trenches.'
*'People's arms*
*sticking out.'*
'Every American
inside.'
'The juggernaut.'
*'I'm not*
*going to sacrifice*
t*he lives*
*of my soldiers*,
Moreno said, *it's not*
*cost-effective.'*
*'The tactic was designed*
*to terrorize*,
Lieutenant Colonel Hawkins
said, who helped
devise it.'
'Schwartzkopf's staff
privately
estimated fifty to seventy
thousand killed
in the trenches.'
'Private Joe Queen was
awarded
a Bronze Star for burying
trenches with his
earthmover.'
'Inside
the juggernaut.'
'Impervious.'
*'A lot of the guys*
*were scared*, he said

*but I*
*enjoyed it.'*
*'A bunch of*
*trenches. People's*
*arms and things*
*sticking out.'*
*'Cost-effective.'*

# In California During the Gulf War

Among the blight-killed eucalypts, among
trees and bushes rusted by Christmas frosts,
the yards and hillsides exhausted by five years of drought,

certain airy white blossoms punctually
reappeared, and dense clusters of pale pink, dark pink –
a delicate abundance. They seemed

like guests arriving joyfully on the accustomed
festival day, unaware of the year's events, not perceiving
the sackcloth others were wearing.

To some of us, the dejected landscape consorted well
with our shame and bitterness. Skies ever-blue,
daily sunshine, disgusted us like smile-buttons.

Yet the blossoms, clinging to thin branches
more lightly than birds alert for flight,
lifted the sunken heart

even against its will.
                    But not
as symbols of hope: they were flimsy
as our resistance to the crimes committed

– again, again – in our name; and yes, they return,
year after year, and yes, they briefly shone with serene joy
over against the dark glare

of evil days. They *are*, and their presence
is quietness ineffable – and the bombings *are*, were,
no doubt will be; that quiet, that huge cacophany

simultaneous. No promise was being accorded, the blossoms
were not doves, there was no rainbow. And when it was claimed
the war had ended, it had not ended.

# In the Land of Shinar

Each day the shadow swings
round from west to east till night overtakes it, hiding
half the slow circle. Each year
the tower grows taller, spiralling
out of its monstrous root-circumference, ramps and colonnades
mounting tier by lessening tier the way a searching
bird of prey wheels and mounts the sky, driven
by hungers unsated by blood and bones.
And the shadow lengthens, our homes nearby are dark
half the day, and the bricklayers, stonecutters, carpenters bivouac
high in the scaffolded arcades, further and further above the ground,
weary from longer and longer comings and goings. At times
a worksong twirls down the autumn leaf of a phrase, but mostly
                                        we catch
only the harsher sounds of their labor itself, and that seems only
an echo now of the bustle and clamor there was long ago
when the fields were cleared, the hole was dug, the foundations laid
with boasting and fanfares, the work begun.
The tower, great circular honeycomb, rises and rises and still
                                the heavens
arch above and evade it, while the great shadow engulfs
more and more of the land, our lives
dark with the fear a day will blaze, or a full-moon night defining
with icy brilliance the dense shade, when all the immense
weight of this wood and brick and stone and metal and massive
weight of dream and weight of will
will collapse, crumble, thunder and fall,
fall upon us, the dwellers in shadow.

# VII The Almost Island

# One December Night...

This I had not expected:
the moon coming right into my kitchen,
the full moon, gently bumping
angles of furniture,
seeming to like the round table
but not resenting corners.

Somehow the moon
filled all the space and yet
left room for whatever
was there already, including me,
and for movement. Like a balloon,
the moon stirred at a breath
and unlike a balloon did not
rise to the ceiling, but wandered
as if sleep-walking,
no more than a foot from the floor.

Music accompanied this lunar visitation –
you would imagine harp or lute, but no,
I'd say it was steel drums,
played with an airy whispering touch.
(Those scooped concavities
might serve as moon-mirrors.)
The greenish tint of white spider-chrysanthemums
resembled the moon's color,
but that was lighter, lighter.

I have been given much, but why this also?
I was abashed. What grand gesture of welcome
was I to make? I bowed, curtsied, but the modest moon
appeared unaware of homage.
I breathed, I gazed; and slowly, mildly,
the moon hovered, touring stove and cupboards,
bookshelves and sink, glimmering
over a bowl of tangerines. And gently
withdrew, just as I thought to summon courage
to offer honey-mead or slivovitz.

# Myopic Birdwatcher

One day the solitary heron,
so tall, so immobile on his usual post,
seemed to have shrunk and grown darker.
Had I imagined
his distinction? Now,
when I wanted my friend to see
what I had seen, it was gone.
And the changed heron had two companions,
somber and hunkered down on neighboring posts.

On succeeding days I saw him again
with and without his doubles,
but even alone he looked shabby, fidgetty,
almost sinister, diminished.
I thought it perhaps a matter
of winter plumage,
seasonal behavior.
Till another friend
came with me to the shore.
'Cormorants,' he said.

It lightened my spirits. My heron's place was usurped,
he disdains to return till they leave –
and they may not leave;
but at least I know
it's not he who,
shrugging his wings to dry them
(a vulgar gesture,
though required, it seems,
by cormorant feathers) displays
the high-shouldered baleful silhouette
of Teutonic eagles on old postage-stamps,
black on a sallow ground
of winter lake-light.
At least I know
I didn't deceive myself:
my absent heron's air of austere dignity
was real, whatever hunger
sustains his watchfulness.

# Mirage

Ethereal mountain,
snowwhite foam hovering
far above blue, cloudy ridges –
can one believe you are not a mirage?

## Against Intrusion

When my friend drove up the mountain
it changed itself into a big
lump of land with lots of snow on it
and slopes of arid scree.
Another friend climbed it the hard way:
exciting to stay the course, get to the top –
but no sense of height there, nothing to see but
generic mist and snow.
As for me,
when my photos come back developed,
there's just the lake, the south shore of the lake,
the middle distance. No mountain.
            How clearly it speaks! *Respect, perspective,*
*privacy,* it teaches. *Indulgence*
*of curiosity increases*
*ignorance of the essential.*
What does it serve to insist
on knowing more than that a mountain,
forbearing – so far – from volcanic rage,
blesses the city it is poised above, angelic guardian
at rest on sustaining air; and that its vanishings
are needful, as silence is to music?

# Looking Through

White as cloud above
a less-white band of cloud
the mountain
stands clear on a sky of
palest blue,
no other clouds in all
the sunny arch
of summer's last holiday.
And the mountain's
deep clefts and hollows,
the shadowy crevasses,
are that same
palest blue, as if
snow and rock,
the whole great mass of mountain,
were transparent
and one could look
through at more sky
southward.
Luminous mountain,
real, unreal sky.

# Whisper

Today the white mist that is weather
is mixed with the sallow tint
of the mist that is smog.
And from it, through it, breathes
a vast whisper:
the mountain.

# Witness

Sometimes the mountain
is hidden from me in veils
of cloud, sometimes
I am hidden from the mountain
in veils of inattention, apathy, fatigue,
when I forget or refuse to go
down to the shore or a few yards
up the road, on a clear day,
to reconfirm
that witnessing presence.

## A Reward

Tired and hungry, late in the day, impelled
to leave the house and search for what
might lift me back to what I had fallen away from,
I stood by the shore waiting.
I had walked in the silent woods:
the trees withdrew into their secrets.
Dusk was smoothing breadths of silk
over the lake, watery amethyst fading to gray.
Ducks were clustered in sleeping companies
afloat on their element as I was not
on mine. I turned homeward, unsatisfied.
But after a few steps, I paused, impelled again
to linger, to look North before nightfall – the expanse
of calm, of calming water, last wafts
of rose in the few high clouds.
And was rewarded:
the heron, unseen for weeks, came flying
widewinged toward me, settled
just offshore on his post,
took up his vigil.
                    If you ask
why this cleared a fog from my spirit,
I have no answer.

## Indian Summer

Zones of flickering
                water-diamonds
converse with almost-still
        glint of leaves along the poplar-row.

A dispersed array of water-birds relaxes
        afloat in autumn light,
one or another sometimes
                        diving casually.

                        And far across
                near the other shore,
        the lake is wearing a narrow, trembling
    band of silver,
a silver barely tinged with gold,
delicate tarnish.

                Someone's tapedeck booms and yells
                crescendo...
                pulses by and zooms
                out of the park.

                And quiet resumes,
                holding off as best it can
                peripheral sounds of human action –
                planes, subliminal traffic,
                (only one motorboat yet,
                it's a workday morning) –

                but admits
        the long and distant old-time wail of a train:
this quiet, this autumn sun,
                cool air and pale
                diaphanous light,
are generous.

# Contrasting Gestures

Coots, heads bobbing, forever urging themselves
fussily onward... How strong their neck-muscles
must be! One is put in mind of human philistines
toiling and spinning through their lives
anxiously complacent in pursuit of trivia.
But coots without warning effortlessly
dive, leaving barely a crease on the black polished-satin
surface – vanishing
into the primal element – !
                              That gesture
of absolute abandon, absolute
release into clear or cloudy
inner flow of the lake: it's what
artists and mystics want to attain, abjuring
acquisition, drunk on occasional
intuitions, on the sense that
*depth, height, breadth* don't express the dimension
which invites them, which evades them...
(Though mystics desire submersion
to transform them, as it does not transform
the coots, who resume
their pushing and nodding forward
after each plunge. And artists
want not themselves transformed
but their work. The plunge itself
their desire, a way to be
subsumed, consumed utterly
into their work.)

# The Almost-Island

The woods which give me their silence,
their ancient Douglas firs and red cedars, their ferns,
are not the wilderness. They're contained
in the two-mile circumference of an almost-island,
a park in city limits. Pleasure-boats crowd at weekends
into the small bay. The veils hiding the mountain
are not always natural cloud. Eagle and heron
speak of solitude, but when you emerge from forest shade
the downtown skyline rears up, phantasmagoric but near,
across the water. Yet the woods, the lake,
the great-winged birds, the vast mountain at the horizon,
are Nature: metonymy of the spirit's understanding
knows them to be a concentrate
of all Thoreau or Wordsworth knew by that word,
Nature: 'a never-failing principle
of joy and purest passion.' Thoreau's own pond
was bounded by the railroad, punctuated
by the 'telegraph trees' and their Aeolian wires.
All of my dread and all of my longing hope that Earth
may outwit the huge stupidity of its humans,
can find their signs and portents here, their recapitulations
of joy and awe. This fine, incised two inches
of goldsmith-work just drifted down, can speak
as well for *tree* as a thousand forest acres,
and tree means depth of roots, uprisen height, outreaching branches.
This musical speech of wavelets jounced against reeds
as a boat's wake tardily reaches the shore,
is *voice of the waters*, voice of all the blue
encircling the terrestrial globe
which as a child I loved to spin
slowly upon its creaking axis – blue globe
we have seen now, round, small as an apple,
afloat in the wilderness we name
so casually, as if we knew it
or ever could know it, 'Space.'

# VIII  The Tide

# After *Mindwalk*

Once we've laboriously
disconnected our old conjunctions –
'physical', 'solid', 'real', 'material' – freed them
from antique measure to admit what,
even through eyes not naked but robed
in optic devices, is not perceptible (oh,
precisely is not perceptible!): admitted
that 'large' and 'small' are bereft
of meaning, since not matter but process, process only,
gathers itself to appear
knowable: *world, universe* –

then what we feel
in moments of bleak arrest,
panic's black cloth falling
over our faces, over our breath,

is a new twist of Pascal's dread,
a shift of scrutiny,
                              its object now
inside our flesh, the *infinite spaces* discovered
within our own atoms, inside the least
particle of what we supposed
our mortal selves (and *in* and *out*side,
what are they?) – its object now

bits of the Void left over from before
the Fiat Lux, immeasurably
incorporate in our discarnate, fictive,
(yes, but sentient,) notion of substance,
inaccurate as our language,
flux which the soul alone
pervades, elusive but persistent.

# Namings

Three hours wholly absorbed: trying to identify one rainsoaked
wormridden mushroom. And the ducks – bufflehead or goldeneye?

The markings once clearly recognized, a glow or grace clarifies
other matters of doubt. They dive, resurface, I know their name.

'What's the most useful thing I can do for you?' I asked the old poet,
lost and distraite in a new apartment. 'Identify things!' she answered,

'What are these?' An empty frame. A box of buttons.
An ivory paper knife. For the moment nothing makes sense.

The need to know *maenad* from *dryad*, to know when you see the
green drift
of watergrass combed by current, the word you desire is *naiad*.

Sorting. Sifting. The ancient tasks, the hero trials, ways to survive,
ways to grow wise. Taxonomies, need to arrange, need to instruct.

We don't trust the stars. *O bright star –* ! No, look,
it's moving. Afraid to feel delight.

Tonight two. One was a plane, plodding slowly towards the airport.
One was a star, very silvery. It's still there.

# Embracing the Multipede

I. *Embracing the Multipede*

On the dream sidewalk
moving towards you
a caterpillar, shiny, hairless, not cute.
Move it
out of harm's way!
It's ringed like an earthworm,
repulsively fecal in color,
with snail-eyes searching about.
Rescue it!
Footsteps will crush it!
It's not so much
like nothing you've seen before
as it is a mixture
of millipede and scorpion.
It's moving towards you,
not cute.
Offer it
your help! It looks
hostile, it may sting you,
but it's small,
each of the multiple feet
the size of an eyelash,
wavering eyes like pinheads.
It's hairless, shiny, repulsive,
scoop it carefully
into your hands,
take it to safety! Not cute, not cute,
it shrinks as you move to meet it,
don't let it vanish before you have time
to give it your heart, a work of mercy.

## II. *Questioning the Creature*

Where are you going, you
disgusting creature?

It's rumoured
there's a barn, lady,
outside of town,
where anyone may scuttle.

And what would you do there,
vile one?

I'd meet
fellow vile ones, sir,
we'd scuttle, we'd scuttle,
in safety.

And what else, loathsome worm?

God knows.
God would hide in our midst
and we'd seek him.


## III. *Pondering the Creature*

Return to my dreams,
little leper of my heart:

I want to know –
who are you?

What is the pitiful, wormish,
dangerously creeping thing

I must protect?
Is this a trick to lure me

under the stones,
under the punkwood crevices,

insect shanties that harbor
you and your boneless kin?

Why did the servile answer
you made to insults

twist in its glistening
exuded track to claim

God as your intimate,
ready to join

your lowly games,
to seek and be found?


IV. *The Creature Absent: An Underpass*

'Cherish the mystery,'
(a voice responds)
'the mystery of this metamorphic
apparition.
          Does it insidiously
claim your pity? Give it some,
You can spare it.
                Is it treacherous, malevolent?
Give it the benefit
of your ample doubt. You have
no positive evidence
it bites or stings.
Perhaps it has for you
some message,
a talisman brought from whatever distance
it travelled to arrive
at you, you in particular,
you only.'

          Who was speaking?
The creature
was absent, not one shadow
changed shape to mark its trail. Echo
of words remained, as if halloo, halloo,
were sounding in a tunnel.

# What the Figtree Said

Literal minds! Embarrassed humans! His friends
were blushing for Him
in secret; wouldn't admit they were shocked.
They thought Him
petulant to curse me! – yet how could the Lord
be unfair? – so they looked away,
then and now.
But I, I knew that
helplessly barren though I was,
my day had come. I served
Christ the Poet,
who spoke in images: I was at hand,
a metaphor for their failure to bring forth
what is within them (as figs
were *not* within me). They who had walked
in His sunlight presence,
they could have ripened,
could have perceived His thirst and hunger,
His innocent appetite;
they could have offered
human fruits – compassion, comprehension –
without being asked,
without being told of need.
My absent fruit
stood for their barren hearts. He cursed
not me, not them, but
(ears that hear not, eyes that see not)
their dullness, that witholds
gifts *unimagined*.

# Contraband

The tree of knowledge was the tree of reason.
That's why the taste of it
drove us from Eden. That fruit
was meant to be dried and milled to a fine powder
for use a pinch at a time, a condiment.
God had probably planned to tell us later
about this new pleasure.
                          We stuffed our mouths full of it,
gorged on *but* and *if* and *how* and again
*but*, knowing no better.
It's toxic in large quantities; fumes
swirled in our heads and around us
to form a dense cloud that hardened to steel,
a wall between us and God, Who was Paradise.
Not that God is unreasonable – but reason
in such excess was tyranny
and locked us into its own limits, a polished cell
reflecting our own faces. God lives
on the other side of that mirror,
but through the slit where the barrier doesn't
quite touch ground, manages still
to squeeze in – as filtered light,
splinters of fire, a strain of music heard
then lost, then heard again.

# On a Theme by Thomas Merton

'Adam, where are you?'
                    God's hands
palpate darkness, the void
that is Adam's inattention,
his confused attention to everything,
impassioned by multiplicity, his despair.

Multiplicity, his despair;
                    God's hands
enacting blindness. Like a child
at a barbaric fairgrounds –
noise, lights, the violent odors –
Adam fragments himself. The whirling rides!

Fragmented Adam stares.
                    God's hands
unseen, the whirling rides
dazzle, the lights blind him. Fragmented,
he is not present to himself. God
suffers the void that is his absence.

## Salvator Mundi: Via Crucis

Maybe He looked indeed
much as Rembrandt envisioned Him
in those small heads that seem in fact
portraits of more than a model.
A dark, still young, very intelligent face,
a soul-mirror gaze of deep understanding, unjudging.
*That* face, in extremis, would have clenched its teeth
in a grimace not shown in even the great crucifixions.
The burden of humanness (I begin to see) exacted from Him
that He taste also the humiliation of dread,
cold sweat of wanting to let the whole thing go,
like any mortal hero out of his depth,
like anyone who has taken a step too far
and wants herself back.
The painters, even the greatest, don't show how,
in the midnight Garden,
or staggering uphill under the weight of the Cross,
He went through with even the human longing
to simply cease, to not be.
Not torture of body,
not the hideous betrayals humans commit
nor the faithless weakness of friends, and surely
not the anticipation of death (not then, in agony's grip)
was Incarnation's heaviest weight,
but this sickened desire to renege,
to step back from what He, Who was God,
had promised Himself, and had entered
time and flesh to enact.
Sublime acceptance, to be absolute, had to have welled
up from those depths where purpose
drifted for mortal moments.

# Ascension

Stretching Himself as if again,
    through downpress of dust
        upward, soil giving way
to thread of white, that reaches
    for daylight, to open as green
        leaf that it is...
Can Ascension
    not have been
        arduous, almost,
as the return
    from Sheol, and
        back through the tomb
into breath?
    Matter reanimate
        now must relinquish
itself, its
    human cells,
        molecules, five
senses, linear
    vision endured
        as Man –
the sole
    all-encompassing gaze
        resumed now,
Eye of Eternity.
    Relinquished, earth's
        broken Eden.
Expulsion,
    liberation,
        last
self-enjoined task
    of Incarnation.
        He again
Fathering Himself.
    Seed-case
        splitting,
He again
    Mothering His birth:
        torture and bliss.

# The Tide

Where is the Giver to whom my gratitude
rose? In this emptiness
there seems no Presence.

*

How confidently the desires
of God are spoken of!
Perhaps God wants
something quite different.
Or nothing, nothing at all.

*

Blue smoke from small
peaceable hearths ascending
without resistance in luminous
evening air.
Or eager mornings – waking
as if to a song's call.
Easily I can conjure
a myriad images
of faith.
Remote. They pass
as I turn a page.

*

Outlying houses, and the train's   rhythm
slows, there's a signal box,
people are taking their luggage
down from the racks.
Then you wake and discover
you have not left
to begin the journey.

*

Faith's a tide, it seems, ebbs and flows responsive
to action and inaction.
Remain in stasis, blown sand
stings your face, anemones
shrivel in rock pools no wave renews.
Clean the littered beach, clear
the lines of a forming poem,
the waters flood inward.
Dull stones again fulfill
their glowing destinies, and emptiness
is a cup, and holds
the ocean.

## Suspended

I had grasped God's garment in the void
but my hand slipped
on the rich silk of it.
The 'everlasting arms' my sister loved to remember
must have upheld my leaden weight
from falling, even so,
for though I claw at empty air and feel
nothing, no embrace,
I have not plummetted.

*Notes*

# A DOOR IN THE HIVE

**To Rilke** (page 16): The allusion is to Rilke's prose piece 'Concerning the Poet' (*Where Silence Reigns*, New Directions).

**To R.D., March 4th 1988** (page 17): Robert Duncan died on 3 February 1988.

**For Instance** (page 21): The German quotation is from the ninth of Rilke's *Duino Elegies*.

**Land of Death Squads** (page 25): My source was a quotation in a review of Jonathan Maslow's *Bird of Life, Bird of Death*. His focus in that book was on Guatemala, where he sought the quetzal in the dwindling forests; but of course the bodies of the 'disappeared' have been found in garbage dumps in other countries as well.

**El Salvador: Requiem and Invocation** (page 26-46): was performed in May 1983 at Sanders Theatre, Harvard University, by the Back Bay Chorale, with soloists, and the Pro Arte Chamber Orchestra, conducted by the late Larry Hill – these two groups having commissioned the work. I had supplied the composer Newell Hendricks with the text in three instalments, and he had worked on the music in that same sequence; the joint project took around a year for us to complete. Until a final rehearsal I did not hear the music, except for a brief orchestral rehearsal tape, as I was in California during the rehearsal period. I had, however, included in my text a few "stage directions", as it were; for in order to meet the challenge of my task at all I had to *imagine* the music in some degree. Thus, with the opening words and phrases I included the suggestion not only that they were for chorus but also that their sounds be loud, harsh, cacophonous; or elsewhere that voices overlap and die away into silence, or perhaps be followed by an orchestral interlude. Newell followed through on all my concepts most intuitively, and produced what I and the audience felt was a very strong and remarkable piece of music.

The basic models in my listening experience were the Bach Passions and various Handel and Haydn oratorios. The Narrator, then, plays a role equivalent to that of the Evangelist in the St Matthew or St. John Passion music. The Chorus represents the people of El Salvador. Occasionally a solo voice emerges from the chorus as an unspecified Questioner. And then there are the solo voices of the Archbishop and the four women.

The narrative line – after the initial outburst of violent words and sounds representing the extremity of El Salvador's present condition – moves from pre-Columbian times through a condensed history of the intervening centuries (which could equally be that of other Central American countries) to very recent events. During the pre-Columbian passages I adapted some actual Mayan prayers; and when I came to contemporary times, I quoted directly from Archbishop Romero's sermons and from the letters by Sisters Dorothy, Maura, and Ita and lay worker Jean, supplied to me by the Maryknoll Sisters. At one point in the text, Romero intones the names of civilians known to have been killed during the previous week: these are actual names, many of them, in this instance, belonging to members (mainly children) of a single family. It is an authentic, typical sampling of those weekly listings of murders done by right-wing death-squads which the Archbishop had the great courage to announce. Similarly, the list, at another point in the text, of priests and nuns murdered in the same manner consists of actual names. It should have been much longer, to be really representative.

The audience at the first performance of the oratorio in 1983 was provided with a program published by the Back Bay Chorale which included the text together with forewords by the composer the conductor, myself, and the artist Michael Mazur who created a visual setting for the event, designed the program cover, and also sang as a member of the Chorale. A new edition was subsequently printed as a contribution to the organisations which are working to help Salvadoran and Guatemalan refugees, develop the ecumenical Covenant of Sanctuary movement, raise public awareness of the true situation, and give medical aid and moral support to the Salvadoran and other Central American people, as well as to protest United States military intervention. Copies were provided free to these organisations (and to a few individuals) for them to sell at whatever price they deemed appropriate.

**Those Who Want Out** (page 51): '...that the earth is an inert lump of matter, that our relationship to it is merely utilitarian, even that we might find a paradise outside it in space colonies. Such monstrous aberrations of thought are symptoms of the enchantment which blinds us to reality.' – John Michell, *The Earth Spirit: Its Ways, Shrines, & Mysteries* (Avon Books, New York, 1975).

# EVENING TRAIN

The poems in Section I, **Lake Mountain Moon** (pages 109-22), were published as a limited edition chapbook by Tangram Press. The poems in Section II, **Two Magnets** (pages 123-30) and several others including **Evening Train**, were written at the Villa Serbelloni, Bellagio, where I spent five weeks in 1989 on a fellowship from the Rockefeller Foundation.

**Stele** (page 126) was inspired by a stone relief in the Musée de Grenoble, France.

The quotations in **The Faithful Lover** (pages 127-28) are all from Ruskin, mainly from *Praeterita*.

**The Composition** (page 130): A duplicate of this painting is in the Boymans Museum in Rotterdam. Witold Rybczinski, in *Home: A Short History of an Idea*, gives a different interpretation of the scene, I discovered. I believe my own is equally valid.

**Entre Loup et Chien** (page 144): the French expression 'entre chien et loup' ('between the dog and the wolf') refers to evening twilight. Here the image is reversed for the predawn twilight.

**News Report, September 1991** (pages 180-82), a found poem, is collaged from *The Seattle Times* of 12 September 1991. To the best of my knowledge it was not followed up and seems to have gone virtually unnoticed in the national media – and the national consciousness.

**After *Mindwalk*** (page 198): *Mindwalk* is a film by Bernt Capra based on writings by Fritjof Capra.

The suite, **Embracing the Multipede** (pages 200-02) was published as a limited edition in chapbook by Tangram Press.

**On a Theme by Thomas Merton** (page 205): the theme alluded to is in one of the tapes of informal lectures given at Gethsemane in the 1960s.

# Index of titles and first lines

(Titles are in italics; first lines in roman type)

# Selected Poems
## DENISE LEVERTOV

This selection spans a thirty-year period, drawn from twelve of Denise Levertov's collections, from *Here and Now* (1957) to *Candles in Babylon* (1982). Her later collections are published separately in Britain by Bloodaxe.

'Denise Levertov is America's foremost contemporary woman poet' – *Library Journal*

'Denise Levertov has evolved a style of her own, clear, sparse, immediate, and vibrant with a very special sensibility and completely feminine insight. She is the most subtly skilful poet of her generation, the most profound, the most modest, the most moving' – KENNETH REXROTH, *New York Times*

'She creates, with great economy, an aura in which something is waiting to shine forth. And it always does. There is a sense in which her poems do not move through time. Her narrative sequences or sequences of images seem to be there all at once, as if remembered, as if divined. This is what creates the hush in which these poems are enveloped – a hush through which we hear and see what is at the heart of the living instant' – ROBERT PACK, *Saturday Review*

'Levertov is a poet of flexibility, depth, and imaginative growth. She has become one of those figures around whom a large part of our sense of what has occurred in American poetry in the last fifteen years or so revolves' – RALPH J. MILLS, *Parnassus*

'For twenty-five years Denise Levertov has been one of our most prominent poets…Today she is a woman at the crest of her maturity, acute in perceptions, wise in responses, and an artist, moreover, whose technique has kept pace with her personal development' – HAYDEN CARRUTH, *1975 Lenhore Marshall Poetry Prize Citation*

'One of the best living poets in America' – JAMES WRIGHT

Paperback: 192 pages ISBN 0 906427 85 1 £8.95

# Oblique Prayers
## DENISE LEVERTOV

In America this new collection was seen as marking a new phase in Denise Levertov's work – more meditative yet still firmly rooted in everyday experience. It includes her translations of 14 poems by the contemporary French poet Jean Joubert.

'Denise Levertov's poetry offers a special voice, clear, spare and utterly skilful: *Oblique Prayers* extends her already wide range. One section probes deeply the individual heart faced with a sense of demanding spirituality; in another I find the first great poetry committed to an awareness of human rights in our time, "political" poetry, disturbing, intensely moving, and poetically true'
– JOHN F. DEANE, *Sunday Independent*

'These recent poems enlarge Levertov's achievement, showing fresh lyrical qualities in her verse. She is a genuine poet with a genuine passion for the life that prevails on the planet' –ALAN BOLD, *Scotsman*

'The first section explores themes which have come to be associated with her – creativity, vision and dream. There are poems which look at the conflict between creativity and love, the desire for the comfort of love to protect against the pain of vision, and the impossibility of such comfort…What makes her political poetry so memorable is its lack of rhetoric, its ability to speak directly and unselfconsciously…There is a bleakness about these poems, an almost overwhelming sense of the lack of love and humanity and hope…The final section moves into the spiritual, perhaps offering something to set against the bleakness of the political poetry. These poems explore the sense of spiritual existence in the beauty of rivers, trees, flowers. The poems capture a tentativeness of vision, a sense of the complexity of the universe, and at the same time an assertion of the spirit, and joy and beauty. *Oblique Prayers* reinforces the fact that Denise Levertov is one of our most important contemporary poets' – CYNTHIA FULLER, *Iron*

Paperback:        80 pages        ISBN 0 906427 89 4        £5.95

# Breathing the Water
## DENISE LEVERTOV

This new collection contains some of Denise Levertov's freshest and most *questioning* poems, as well as some of her most powerful political poems. It takes the reader from public issues back to the most personal, spiritual concerns. The poems are lit with Levertov's spiritual awareness and glow with her joy in the physical world, her awe and wonder in creation. They warn against our failure to respond to that beauty. They tell us *not* to acquiesce, *not* to allow ourselves to be duped or dulled. Levertov's voice is not a lone cry but a call to sanity. To read and hear her in these poems is to share her vision. *Breathing the Water* is a book to give us hope.

'This is a poetry that with personal honesty acknowledges despair and points to the sources of strength and hope with which that despair may be met. It's not just poetry: it's a commitment to "breathing the water", to being human here now' – GILLIAN ALLNUTT, *City Limits*

'Spacious, sane, full of luminosity and musical in a gentle, seamless way, this is the work of a great poet still at the height of her talent' – *Time Out*

'These are the poems of a mature woman, living with their origins and experienced past, gemmed with bright perceptions, passionate with sorrow and anger, full of love and rue for the missing or lost' – ALAN RIACH, *Cencrastus*

'*Breathing the Water* is the sharpest, most affecting critique of Thatcher's England I have ever read...Her range is formidable – elegy, allegory, invective: magical lyricism, imagist precision; philosophical argument, emotional outburst. The most important development for Levertov may be the Christian beliefs and cadences she has begun to speak and live through. I'm surprised I can share her vision without demur' – PETER PEGNALL, *Fortnight*

| Paperback: | 80 pages | ISBN 1 85224 051 2 | £5.95 |

**Denise Levertov** was born in 1923, and grew up in Ilford, Essex. She was educated at home by her Welsh mother and by her father, a Russian Jew who settled in England after the First World War and became an Anglican priest. Her first book of poems, *The Double Image*, was published by the Cresset Press, London, in 1946. Two more collections were published in Britain by Cape, in 1965 and 1968, but nothing else for nearly 20 years; Bloodaxe took over the publication of her work for her UK readership in 1986.

In 1948 she moved to America, and was published in Kenneth Rexroth's anthology *The New British Poets*. 'She, more than anyone,' Rexroth was to write later, 'led the redirection of American poetry …to the mainstream of world literature.' During the next three decades she became 'America's foremost contemporary woman poet' (*Library Journal*). She continued to work also as a political activist, campaigning for civil rights, against the Vietnam War, against the Bomb, and against US-backed régimes in Latin America. 'We are living our whole lives in a state of emergency,' she wrote in 1967.

All Levertov's books are published by New Directions in the States. Her first nine American collections are available in *Collected Earlier Poems 1940-1960, Poems 1960-1967* and *Poems 1968-1972*. Also available are the separate collections *The Freeing of the Dust* (1975), *Life in the Forest* (1978) and *Candles in Babylon* (1982). Poems from all these collections are included in her British *Selected Poems*, published by Bloodaxe in 1986. Her later collections are separately available from New Directions in the States and from Bloodaxe in Britain: *Oblique Prayers* (USA 1984/UK 1986), *Breathing the Water* (USA 1987/UK 1988), *A Door in the Hive* (USA 1989) and *Evening Train* (USA 1992), the latter two collections published in Britain as one book by Bloodaxe in 1993.

She has also published translations of two French poets: Guillevic's *Selected Poems* (New Directions) and Jean Joubert's *Black Iris* (Copper Canyon Press). New Directions have also published her prose books *The Poet in the World* (1973) and *Light Up the Cave* (1982), and the currently available *New & Selected Essays* (1992).